Creative Nonfiction in S[Exercise Research

Academics around the world recognise the effectiveness of storytelling as a way to engage audiences in conversations, raising awareness of issues, and encouraging change. Stories are now seen as the best medium to convey information to diverse audiences.

This book explores a novel approach to representing research findings through the adoption of creative nonfictional stories (CNF). At a time when dissemination of scientific research is constantly highlighted as a fundamental aspect for academics, CNF represents an opportunity to effectively communicate science to non-academic audiences through stories.

By providing practical examples of how to transform findings into compelling stories rooted in data, following the mantra of showing rather than telling, which characterises CNF, *Creative Nonfiction in Sport and Exercise Research* helps researchers – qualitative, quantitative, established professors, and students – to turn their research into stories.

A unique contribution to the field, this book is the first in the sport and exercise research field to take scholars on a discovery journey, moving from their classic realist tales to a more creative, compelling, but still rigorous representation of research findings. The book features chapters written by authors from different sport research backgrounds, who present the findings of a previously published 'classic' study rewritten in the form of a story. Reflective chapters focusing on the how-to and the challenges of this creative analytical practice complete the work, to support scholars in developing their creative skills.

Francesca Cavallerio is a Senior Lecturer in Sport and Exercise Psychology in the School of Psychology and Sport Science at Anglia Ruskin University, UK.

Qualitative Research in Sport and Physical Activity

Series Editors:
Michael D. Giardina, Florida State University, USA
Brett Smith, Durham University, UK

From ethnography and narrative inquiry to participatory action research and digital methods, feminist and poststructural theory to new materialism and onto-epistemologies, serious conversations about the practices, politics and philosophies of qualitative inquiry have never been stronger or more abundant in the field of sport, exercise and health. At the same time, the growth of new critical methodologies has opened up interdisciplinary space for sustained engagement with provocative questions over evidence, knowledge, and research practices. The *Qualitative Research in Sport and Physical Activity* series is the first of its kind within the field that has as its mandate the necessary advancement of qualitative methodologies and their intersection with theory and practice. Books in the series will develop new and innovative methodologies, serve as 'how-to' guides for conducting research, and present empirical research findings. It will serve the growing number of students and academics who promote and utilize qualitative inquiry in university courses, research, and applied practice.

Also available in this series:

Physical Culture, Ethnography and the Body
Theory, method and praxis
Edited by Michael D. Giardina and Michele K. Donnelly

Sport, Politics and the Charity Industry
Running for Water
Kyle Bunds

Digital Qualitative Research in Sport and Physical Activity
Edited by Andrea Bundon

Creative Nonfiction in Sport and Exercise Research
Edited by Francesca Cavallerio

www.routledge.com/sport/series/QRSPA

Creative Nonfiction in Sport and Exercise Research

Edited by
Francesca Cavallerio

Routledge
Taylor & Francis Group

NEW YORK AND LONDON

First published 2022
by Routledge
605 Third Avenue, New York, NY 10158

and by Routledge
2 Park Square, Milton Park, Abingdon, Oxon, OX14 4RN

Routledge is an imprint of the Taylor & Francis Group, an informa business

© 2022 Taylor & Francis

Library of Congress Cataloging-in-Publication Data
A catalog record for this title has been requested

ISBN: 978-0-367-48266-4 (hbk)
ISBN: 978-1-032-12016-4 (pbk)
ISBN: 978-1-003-03890-0 (ebk)

DOI: 10.4324/9781003038900

Typeset in Times New Roman
by codeMantra

To my family,
   For always supporting me in writing my own story.
   Thank you

Contents

Figures

Contributors

Jacquelyn Allen-Collinson
University of Lincoln, Lincoln UK

Francesca Cavallerio
Anglia Ruskin University, UK

Charles L.T. Corsby
Cardiff Metropolitan University, UK

Melissa Day
University of Chichester, UK

Adam B. Evans
University of Copenhagen, Denmark

Niels Boysen Feddersen
The Norwegian University of Science and Technology, Norway

Chris G. Harwood
Loughborough University, UK

Gretchen Kerr
University of Toronto, Canada

Camilla J. Knight
Swansea University, UK

Laura Martinelli
University of Chichester, UK

Kerry R. McGannon
Laurentian University, Canada

Jenny McMahon
University of Tasmania, Australia

Gareth McNarry
Loughborough University, UK

Rebecca Palmer
Anglia Ruskin University, UK

Anna Stodter
Anglia Ruskin University, UK

Ross Wadey
St Mary's University, UK

Erin Willson
University of Toronto, Canada

Foreword

I have been fascinated by creative nonfiction (CNF) for over two decades. I was introduced to this creative analytical practice during my MSc in 1995 and in 1999, the year my PhD began, I published my first one. I've published several CNFs since then.

Despite *my* interest in CNF, it would be wrong to suggest that this type of creative analytical practice has gained huge interest across the sport and exercise sciences. There are many reasons for this. These include the perception that CNF is not 'proper research'. I suspect another reason is that we have not had enough concerted efforts to bring together CNFs within one place. A book that does this is therefore one necessary move forward.

Bringing together CNFs within a book provides audiences with a rich set of rationales for why CNF can be useful. These rationales should not simply be crafted through a series of tellings – 'let me tell you, the reader, why CFN is important through a set of monologues and reasoned arguments…'. The reasons why CNF needs to be taken seriously by all sport and exercise scientists, irrespective of their discipline, should also be *shown* through *multiple acts of storytelling*.

Why? Stories provide valuable insights into people's meaning-making, experiences, materiality, and psycho-socio-cultural worlds. But stories can also function as highly effective forms of communication and persuasion. They can communicate complex knowledge in ways that are highly accessible to different audiences, not just academics. This makes CNFs a highly attractive proposition for the increasing number of researchers across the sport and exercise sciences – and beyond – who want the knowledge from their research translated effectively to the public.

Research communicated through storytelling, just like a good CNF does, is also appealing when we consider impact. That impact can include raising awareness, creating new understandings, changing behaviour, improving professional practice, supporting health and well-being, advancing policy, and challenging troubling practices. Stories are not miracle workers, but they can help drive such change because stories have various capacities. They have the capacity to make research compelling and enact truths. They also perform and arouse people's imagination.

Stories perform by doing things on, to, and with people. They can attract people, hold their attention, and work their ways into people's flesh, changing what they think and how they act. Stories also reassemble what is always drifting apart, thereby enacting or performing memory. Stories further rouse imagination and through imagination stories arouse emotions. Emotions are powerful, affecting how we think, feel, and might behave. Working with stories thus opens many opportunities up for sport and exercise scientists.

It is with great delight then that I have the honour of writing this foreword to a book that opens up so much. Expertly edited by Dr Francesca Cavallerio, this book dares to bring data, analysis, theory, and storytelling together through the genre of CNF. It does not simply *tell* readers about CNF and what this creative analytical practice might do. It *shows* readers what CNF can offer. In so doing, not only does this book add important knowledge to our field and push researchers to think differently about how they might communicate their research results, but it is also hoped the collection of research-driven stories expands our repertoire of narrative resources to work with. It is hoped that a book which brings together CNF ambushes readers, stirs their imagination, gets under their skin, and calls on them to act in ways that benefit the people, groups, and communities they work with.

I hope readers will appreciate the book as much as I did. Like concentric circles of witness, it is hoped that this book teaches, reaches different audiences, makes a difference, and opens up possible new worlds. Enjoy!

Brett Smith
Durham University

Acknowledgements

I would like to thank all the authors who contributed to this book, for their time, work, and enthusiasm in participating in this project, despite these challenging times.

In particular, I would like to thank Ross Wadey for the inspirational conversation we had in front of the library at St Mary's University a couple of years ago, which sparked the idea for this book. I look forward to many more lovely chats in the future.

.

Introduction

Francesca Cavallerio

A beach. A calm, blue, sparkling sea. The sun, warm and high in the clean sky.

A blonde, skinny, 11-year-old, sitting on a rock, closing a book, a satisfied smile on her face. *What a good story! Pity it's finished.*

"I will become a writer one day!", I exclaim, beaming.

DAD: "A writer? That's interesting… Why do you want to be one?"

"Yes, isn't it? I want to write stories, stories about people's lives. Look at that fisherman," I point towards a drifting boat, "I bet he has an interesting life. With lots of adventures! Imagine how amazing it would be to capture those stories…," I go on, a glimmer in my eyes.

DAD: "Ok…but - you know - people normally don't start their career just as writers. It is usually a part-time job…you need to be really good and famous to just do that, full-time…"

"Aw…ok…well, no problem. I will be a journalist for the rest of the time then," I say, looking adoringly a few rocks to our left, where Sara, my mum's friend, sits. She is a journalist and I think she is awesome. I want to be like her, which makes being a journalist just perfect.

DAD: "…mmm…well…it's just that usually it is the same for journalists…it usually starts as a part-time job…it's not so easy to 'make it,' like Sara for example."

I look at him, silently. I don't see the problem.

"It is perfect then. I will be a part-time writer and a part-time journalist!"

DAD: looks at me for a second, he smiles, "…good luck eating." He chuckles and walks away, amused by his little girl's dreams.

***

DOI: 10.4324/9781003038900-1

[20 years later, Spring 2015]

Subject: Realist tales

"Dear Ross and Chris,
I tried to represent the ethnography findings using a realist tale, but it feels too clinical to me; I don't think it works. I was wondering if you thought I could try and represent them using this more adventurous way that I was reading about…it is called 'creative nonfiction'…could I give it a go? Do you think it would be a possibility for my first study?"

Subject: Re: Realist Tales:
"[…] It might be better to stick to something more 'classic' for your PhD, why don't you send us the realist tale, and then we can see what to do."

Subject: Re: Re: Realist Tale:
"Ok, no problem. See attached."

Subject: Re: Re: Re: Realist Tale:
"Fran, you were right. The finding section is very long and boring, yes. Ok, let's do this. Why don't you give a go to the creative nonfiction? Let's see if like you said it could work better, maybe help you represent the complexity of your findings."

And there it was. My turning point. That moment where your previously imagined life – the 11-year-old life – started to merge with the real, actual, this-is-your-life-as-a-grown-up life. The moment I realised that stories *can be* part of an academic's life, and not just 'part' of it, they can be at the core of one's work. I smiled, reminded of my fascination for that fisherman's adventurous life, how entertaining I thought it could be. Yet, stories can do so much more. They can be a key to *understand* people and to *reach* them (Frank, 2010).

Stories, Science, and Qualitative Research

Well, look at me, finally! My first job! It is nice of my colleague to suggest she'd introduce me and my research to the students before I teach the qualitative sessions on the module.

"Dr Fran Cavallerio is a new member of staff and a 'qually' researcher. Fran does research in sport psychology, and she writes *stories* for her research."

Mm. This seems nice but…is it me being hypersensitive or that sounded a little condescending?

"She will be teaching you qually stuff towards the end of the module. But for the first weeks, I will be looking at data and stats with you."

"Well, we will be looking at data as well, don't worry." *Is that my voice? Did I really interrupt her?*

"Yes, of course. It was just to help the students get the difference between quantitative research, with facts and stats, and qually, with words and stories."

It's definitely there. I am not imagining that tone. Look at the students, look at their puzzled faces: the new, artsy, member of staff. Not only a qualitative researcher, but one who writes stories. How do I tackle this situation?

"Well, let's put it this way: you guys stay strong for the next few weeks, and then when I meet you, we will debunk a few myths on qualitative research, and I'll try and show you why '*writing stories*' is not just a way to write up findings, but it can be a way of doing research according to certain approaches, values, and beliefs. I look forward to discussing these with you." I turn towards my colleague with an innocent smile plastered on my face and let her continue with the module introduction.

In Italy we grow up used to Dante's famous expression, "Don't mind them but walk on by!",[1] and I tried to follow the same guidance in that classroom. But I couldn't stop thinking, there it was, the clash, the dichotomy I often read about in books (e.g., Smith, 2013a). Barone (2008) explains how the well-known polar opposite characters of 'the scientist' (i.e., white coat, lab-based, rigorous, able to approach a definite, reassuring, 'objective truth') and the 'literary/artistic intellectual' (i.e., crumpled clothes, gaze lost somewhere on the horizon, non-methodical approach to life, fan of creativity and diversity) still exist today, and – too often – still struggle to coexist.

The dichotomy fact/fiction, then, reflects these two cultures, and is often simply assumed as being 'what' these two cultures should produce. Scientists produce facts, artists produce fiction. Yet, over the past two decades, a puzzling term appeared, one that is in itself an oxymoron (i.e., a figure of speech, which seems self-contradictory): *creative nonfiction*. As Foster Wallace (2014) explained,

> As nonfiction, the works are connected to actual states of affairs in the world, are "true" to some reliable extent. If, for example, a certain event is alleged to have occurred, it must really have occurred; if a proposition is asserted, the reader expects some proof of (or argument for) its accuracy. At the same time, the adjective *creative* signifies that some goal(s) other than sheer truthfulness motivates the writer and informs her work […] *Creative* also suggests that this kind of nonfiction tends to bear traces of its own artificing; the essay's author usually wants us to see and understand her as the text's maker.
>
> (p. 1)

Descartes' distinction of mind and body is often at the heart of rigid, dualistic conceptualisations in the Western culture, and the juxtapositions of science and art, and of fact and fiction are nothing but examples of this process (Hanrahan, 2003). The 17th century saw an "assault on ambiguity" (Barone, 2008, p. 106) with mathematical and physical sciences emphasising the importance of theoretical rigour and metric precision. Nonetheless, examples of transgression soon developed – possibly a sign that such dualism does not exist, surely not in such extreme terms as described by Descartes – and the boundaries between fact and fiction were up for discussion once again. Through the centuries social scientists and writers kept playing with these boundaries, pushing (past) them and exploring different possibilities (e.g., Emile Zola's social realist novels; Barone, 2008). According to Pauly (2014), New Journalism developed in the 1960s through discussions about the line between reporting facts and telling fiction and the role of interpretation in news reporting. Soon these conversations were echoed inside the walls of academia, as several scholars (e.g., Elliot Eisner, Clifford Geertz, Norman Denzin, Carolyn Ellis, Laurel Richardson to name only a few) started questioning the dominant ideas in human sciences on how to describe social reality, and how to effectively capture lived experiences (Sparkes, 1995). The crisis of representation generated a quest for different ways to represent research, give voice to participants, and explore the consequences and possibilities that blurring the line between fact and fiction could bring (Barone, 2008). Creative nonfiction was among those 'new' *creative analytical practices* (Richardson, 2000).

For the field of sport and exercise, the revolutionary approaches to representing research were brought to the attention of scholars by Andrew Sparkes' (1995, 2002) work. Sparkes (1995) highlighted the need – and possibility – for writing research in different ways, exploring how different tales would offer a different representation of *voice* (i.e., the author's, the participants'). Over the years, a number of scholars started to adopt creative nonfiction to represent their research (e.g., Blodgett, Ge, Schinke, & McGannon, 2017; Carless & Sparkes, 2008; Cavallerio, Wadey, & Wagstaff, 2016; Richardson & Motl, 2021; Smith, 2013b), yet many researchers are still discouraged by the craft of writing creatively, or uncomfortable playing in the space between fact and fiction.

Learning the Craft of Creative Nonfiction

What is the craft of creative nonfiction writing based on, then? How can we learn this 'craft'? How can we make it less daunting for academics? These were the questions running around in my head when I first started working on this book. I always dreamt of writing; I cannot recall a time of my life when I wasn't writing a story. My childhood room is still bursting with bigger and smaller notebooks – my mum recently complained about finding 'another one!' – and they are full of the beginning of one story or another. Writing always fascinated me, which helps me understand why I felt comfortable enough years ago to ask my supervisors to let me try something new and different. Yet, if a person is less comfortable with writing, then the boundaries and rules of scientific tales must have a reassuring quality, and the mere idea of creative writing might be scary. Nonetheless, it is a skill that everyone can try, learn, and refine. Most importantly no researcher will ever completely 'start from scratch' when it comes to creative nonfiction, according to one of the main experts in the field, Lee Gutkind.

Gutkind (1996) explains that creative nonfiction is based on what he calls '*the 5 Rs*': Real-life immersion, Reflection, Research, Reading, and 'Riting (I know, cheeky). By breaking down creative nonfiction into these five areas, researchers might start feeling the flicker of hope that this challenge might be achievable. The more I read Gutkind's editorial piece, the more I think those involved in academic life (e.g., students, ECRs, experienced academics) might almost consider themselves privileged, because the 5 Rs are (or should be) part of their everyday approach to their work as qualitative researchers. When conducting most of the research, we do immerse ourselves in real-life situations (first R), with some methodological approaches encouraging this aspect more than others (e.g., ethnography). Also, when interviewing, we still aim to immerse ourselves to gain an understanding of our participants' experiences and worlds.

Reflection, Gutkind's second R, should also be a skill refined through our work as qualitative researchers. Reflexivity and researcher's positionality are discourses that have been encouraged since the crisis of representation, over the past three decades (Mayan, 2016) and their development has played a fundamental role in the improvement of the quality of qualitative research. Gutkind (1996) goes on explaining that,

> The second reason Creative Nonfiction and most other journals and magazines reject essays is a lack of attention to the mission of the genre, which is to gather and present information, to teach readers about a person, place, idea or situation combining the creativity of the artistic experience with [...] research.
>
> (p. 1)

What Gutkind refers to as doing research is actually gathering information, i.e., collecting data. Therefore, academics should be safe from this perspective. What I mean is that, once we get to deciding what tale to use to represent our findings, we already have Gutkind's third R "in the bag," so to speak, because we have the data (i.e., the nonfiction). The quality of such data will of course depend on several aspects, but the need for research as a key aspect of writing creative nonfiction should not be what discourages us, because it is part of the academic research process.

The next R, reading, is a natural consequence of the research, but it also is the point where academics might need to put some work in. Of course, we need to read about our topic area to inform our research. But we also need to read – just read, not review – examples of the type of writing we want to attempt. Read the great writers, and just read – fiction and nonfiction – and ask yourself what you are enjoying of one book or another. Is it the style? Is it the plot? Is it the pace, the narrative perspective? What makes you rush through a novel, unable to put it down, and what makes you abandon it halfway? To engage in writing creative nonfiction, the more examples you have to draw upon, the easier it will be.

Now onto the final R: 'riting. I enjoy how Gutkind summarises the previous Rs as the nonfiction work, and then describes 'riting as "the most artistic and romantic aspect of the whole experience" (p. 2). It comes with its joys – those inspired moments where time is still, and your fingertips are tapping away, rushing through the keyboard, or wrapped tightly around a pen, scribbling idea after idea on a piece of paper, feeling the pain in your hand but not able to stop – and its dull, laborious moments, when writing requires planning, schedules, a daily or weekly grind. It is with the challenges of this final R in mind that this book has been written.

Why This Book?

Over the past few years, there has been a growing interest in the 'impact' of research, and in the process of 'knowledge translation' (Graham et al., 2006), aiming to bridge the gap between scientific research and everyday life. Scientists can continue to develop their work in amazing ways, but we have become more and more aware that knowledge is useless if people do not have a chance to understand it. A well-structured, novel, peer-reviewed paper might look good on one's curriculum vitae, but it will not change the world we live in if the people who live in this world are not in a position to understand what it says.

This is where stories started to play a role of growing importance. We are *storytelling animals*, naturally drawn to stories (Gottschall, 2012). Bruner (1991) explained how humans organise their experience and their memory of events in the form of narrative, be it a story, a myth, an excuse. Creative nonfiction is one way of writing stories, and as such, it offers researchers one way of sharing results from systematic and rigorous research in a 'language' that reaches further than the academic community (Smith, McGannon, & Williams, 2016). Stories also have the power to change us, inspire us, make us reflect, and become more aware, and they do so by engaging our brains, mainly through emotions (Aldama, 2015). Zak (2015) explains how the production of oxytocin in our brain in response to a story reflects our level of empathy and can predict prosocial behaviours (Zak, Stanton, & Ahmadi, 2007).

There is not a right or a wrong way of writing creative nonfiction. There might be ways that are more or less effective, and there are certainly several skills that might not come naturally and need to be honed, characteristics of this type of writing that one has to study and develop. Yet, there is also the experience of writing as 'infiltrating' research, in the way we think, read, and write our own work. There is the beauty of creativity, the sense of freedom. Daunting at times, but also liberating, as the authors in this book recounted when asked about their experience (see Chapter 10).

Therefore, the aim of this book is to encourage researchers to consider and explore – even play with – creative nonfiction as a possible way to represent their research. The book wants to be a companion in this process, and an encouraging one. It is here to show how creative nonfiction can be developed, to highlight the differences from a 'classic,' realist tale (Sparkes, 2002), and to provide the reader with examples of different approaches and ways of writing and structuring creative nonfiction. Some will resonate and connect more than others, depending on personal taste and interests – after all, we do not all enjoy reading the same books. This book is also empirical, in the way it adds to the research base, because of the layer of analysis that happens through writing (Richardson, 2000). The creative nonfictions presented in the following chapters add nuance and insight to issues previously raised, and now represented in a new light. I hope that, in one way or another, it might inspire and pave the way for more researchers to experiment and explore how to share research in ways that can be enjoyed by audiences both in and outside academia.

Structure of the Book

The book is organised in three parts. The first part aims to offer some guidance on the process of writing creative nonfiction to represent research findings. *Chapter 1* focuses on 'unpacking' the well-known and deceivingly simple '*show rather than tell*' mantra of CNF, by analysing the literary techniques that are fundamental in this process. *Chapter 2* offers an example of work in progress, moving from realist tale to the first storying attempt, to the final product. Allowing readers the opportunity to examine how the same story can be portrayed and re-written through different stages, this chapter aims to support researchers in the practicalities of writing.

The second part of the book presents a series of chapters that exemplify a variety of approaches to writing creative nonfiction. The authors of these chapters have been invited to select a previously published peer-reviewed study, written up using the form of a realist tale, and to rewrite their results using creative nonfiction. Browsing through the chapters, readers will be able to observe how the same information might be communicated in a different way, and what new layers might have been uncovered by the authors through their writing. Questions at the end of each chapter can be used as prompts for further reflection. The variety of topics and disciplines from the field of Sport and Exercise research also aims to highlight how creative nonfiction can be used to address different areas. *Chapter 3* looks at experiences of parenting in sport, while *Chapter 4* specifically focuses on the negotiation of the identities of athlete and mother, and *Chapter 5* presents the concept of 'positive pain' in competitive swimming. *Chapters 6* and *7* move the focus to coaches and their experiences of learning and developing athletes. Finally, *Chapters 8 and 9* bring our attention to the dark side of sport, respectively discussing being in a destructive organisational culture and portraying stories of emotional abuse in elite sport.

Lastly, the final part of the book presents some reflections on doing creative nonfiction and challenges the idea of a one-size-fits-all approach. *Chapter 10* uses data collected from the authors who contributed to the chapters in Part II to reflect on the experience of engaging with writing creative nonfiction and does so by proposing a mixed approach to representation, reflecting on its possible benefits. Almost taking the opposite approach, *Chapter 11* opens up further possibilities for representing creative nonfiction, encouraging researchers to move beyond the limits of the written word.

Acknowledgement

I would like to thank Charlie Corsby for his thought-provoking comments on the initial version of this Introduction.

Note

1 Dante Alighieri, the most famous Italian poet, who wrote the "Divine Comedy" and uses this expression in *Canto III*, where the poet Virgil encourages Dante to continue walking, without paying attention to those people not worth of it.

References

Aldama, F. L. (2015). The science of storytelling: Perspectives from cognitive science, neuroscience, and the humanities. *Projections*, *9*(1), 80–95. https://doi.org/10.3167/proj.2015.090106

Barone, T. (2008). Creative nonfiction and social research. In G. Knowles & A. Cole (Eds.), *Handbook of the arts in qualitative research* (pp. 105–115). Thousand Oaks, CA: Sage.

Blodgett, A. T., Ge, Y., Schinke, R. J., & McGannon, K. R. (2017). Intersecting identities of elite female boxers: Stories of cultural difference and marginalization in sport. *Psychology of Sport and Exercise, 32*, 83–92. https://doi.org/10.1016/j.psychsport.2017.06.006

Bruner, J. (1991). The narrative construction of reality. *Critical Inquiry, 18*(1), 1–21.

Carless, D., & Sparkes, A. C. (2008). The physical activity experiences of men with serious mental illness: Three short stories. *Psychology of Sport and Exercise, 9*(2), 191–210. https://doi.org/10.1016/j.psychsport.2007.03.008

Cavallerio, F., Wadey, R., & Wagstaff, C. R. (2016). Understanding overuse injuries in rhythmic gymnastics: A 12-month ethnographic study. *Psychology of Sport and Exercise, 25*, 100–109. https://doi.org/10.1016/j.psychsport.2016.05.002

Frank, A. W. (2010). *Letting stories breathe: A socio-narratology.* Chicago, IL: University of Chicago Press.

Gottschall, J. (2012). *The storytelling animal: How stories make us human.* Boston, NY: Houghton Mifflin Harcourt.

Graham, I. D., Logan, J., Harrison, M. B., Straus, S. E., Tetroe, J., Caswell, W., & Robinson, N. (2006). Lost in knowledge translation: Time for a map? *Journal of Continuing Education in the Health Professions, 26*(1), 13–24.

Gutkind, L. (1996). From the editor: The 5 Rs of creative nonfiction. *Creative Nonfiction*, 1–14.

Hanrahan, M. (2003). Challenging the dualistic assumptions of academic writing: Representing Ph.D. research as embodied practice. In *Forum qualitative sozialforschung* (Vol. 4, No. 2, pp. 1–16). Institut fur Klinische Sychologie and Gemeindesychologie.

Mayan, M. J. (2016). *Essentials of qualitative inquiry.* Abingdon: Routledge.

Pauly, J. J. (2014). The new journalism and the struggle for interpretation. *Journalism, 15*(5), 589–604. https://doi.org/10.1177/1464884914529208

Richardson, E., & Motl, R. W. (2021). 'Kicking and screaming" or 'gracefully conceding': Creative nonfiction stories of aging with multiple sclerosis. *Qualitative Health Research.* https://doi.org/10.1177/10497323211009864

Richardson, L. (2000). Writing: A method of inquiry. In N. K. Denzin & Y. S. Lincoln (Eds.), *Handbook of qualitative research* (2nd ed., pp. 923–948). Thousand Oaks, CA: Sage.

Smith, B. (2013a). Artificial persons and the academy. In N. P. Short, L. Turner, & A. Grant (Eds.), *Contemporary British autoethnography* (pp. 187–202). Rotterdam: Sense Publishers.

Smith, B. (2013b). Sporting spinal cord injuries, social relations, and rehabilitation narratives: An ethnographic creative non-fiction of becoming disabled through sport. *Sociology of Sport Journal, 30*(2), 132–152. https://doi.org/10.1123/ssj.30.2.132

Smith, B., McGannon, K. R., & Williams, T. L. (2016). Ethnographic creative nonfiction. In G. Molnár & L. Purdy (Eds.), *Ethnographies in sport and exercise research* (pp. 49–73). Abingdon: Routledge.

Sparkes, A. C. (1995). Writing people: Reflections on the dual crises of representation and legitimation in qualitative inquiry. *Quest, 47*(2), 158–195. https://doi.org/10.1080/00336297.1995.10484151

Sparkes, A. C. (2002). *Telling tales in sport and physical activity: A qualitative journey.* Champaign, IL: Human Kinetics Publishers.

Wallace, D. F. (2014). *The David Foster Wallace Reader.* New York: Hachette Book Group.

Zak, P. J. (2015, January). Why inspiring stories make us react: The neuroscience of narrative. In *Cerebrum: The Dana forum on brain science* (Vol. 2015). Dana Foundation.

Zak, P. J., Stanton, A. A., & Ahmadi, S. (2007). Oxytocin increases generosity in humans. *PLoS One, 2*(11), e1128. https://doi.org/10.1371/journal.pone.0001128

Part I
Learning the Craft of Creative Nonfiction

1 'Where Do I Start?'

Getting to Grips with Creative Nonfiction

Francesca Cavallerio

Show Rather Than Tell

'Hello Ma'am, what would you like?'

The voice of the young guy behind the counter snaps me out of the reverie state I had been lulled into while queueing. I stare at the board behind him, quickly deciding.

'A mocha, please'

'Mocha, great. And where will you be sitting?'

'Mmmm…– I turn, looking around the open-space coffee shop, almost holding my breath, and…yes! It's free! – I'll be there', I say, pointing to one of my favourite corners: two armchairs and a low table, encased in between the wall, a small pillar, and the full-height window. Quiet but light, it's perfect!

I pay and then brusquely walk to my corner before someone else snatches it. I sit down and feel my lips stretching into a smile. It might seem petty, but now I feel I can have a good working morning. One of the perks of life in academia, something that my students are still puzzled about…the 'working-from-home day', which in my case often means 'find a nice coffee shop with good coffee and work.'

My mocha arrives, warm and chocolatey, my laptop is open in front of me. Let's get the day started! I am meeting Luke in half an hour, so I really need to review his first attempt at a creative nonfiction.

Object: Brief first attempt at story.

Click-click. Aw. Indeed. It IS brief.

I stare at the page and a half in front of me.

Three bulky paragraphs.

Breathe in.

It all began playing in the back garden when I was really young, almost as soon as I could stand up by myself, I would be holding a bat. I was always throwing and hitting balls around and quickly I grew attached. I developed a real passion for cricket, my parents took me down to the local cricket club and I started playing and making friends until eventually the club became my second home.

DOI: 10.4324/9781003038900-3

Colts cricket really starts around the age of 11 where you begin to play with a hard ball, you're playing for club, at school and if you are chosen to, you even get the opportunity to be involved with a representative side.

[...]

The men's leagues were a lot bigger in terms of geographical location. I was familiar with travelling a bit with my county in the age groups but that was with parents, driving yourself is a whole different ball game and the cricket itself a whole new ballpark. It was no longer a pleasant environment. To gain an understanding of how much teams wanted to win you only need to know how much some players are being paid. Along with this comes peer pressure, peer pressure from team mates to play week-in-week-out and if you don't, well you better have had a great excuse for not playing because you'd know about it on return [...].[1]

Okay.

What do I do now? I don't want to crush his enthusiasm, but this is WAY away from being a creative nonfiction. It bears no semblance at all. It is so descriptive, so tedious! Did he read the paper and the chapter I sent him? Where is the emotion? Nowhere is he showing anything...this is a list...how do we turn a list into a story? I should have never suggested this. If I turn him back towards writing a realist tale, it will look like I don't believe in him. But...can *this* become good enough not to ruin his dissertation?!

DLIN!

'Hey, Emma!'

Luke is standing at the door, waving. He is early. Smiling. Eager to work.

Ok, then. Let's work on this.

How did *I* learn to write CNF?

* * *

[*Two years before*]

As the play begins, it is raining quite heavily. **Mag Folan**, *a stoutish woman in her early seventies with short, tightly permed grey hair and a mouth that gapes slightly, is sitting in the rocking chair, staring off into space. Her left hand is somewhat more shrivelled and red than her right. The front door opens and her daughter,* **Maureen**, *a plain, slim woman of about forty, enters carrying shopping and goes through to the kitchen.*

MAG: Wet, Maureen?
MAUREEN: Of course wet.
MAG: Oh-h.

MAUREEN: *takes her coat off, sighing, and starts putting the shopping away.*
MAG: I did take me Complan.
MAUREEN: So you can get it yourself so.
MAG: I can. (*Pause.*) Although lumpy it was, Maureen.
MAUREEN: Well, can I help lumpy?
MAG: No.

The Beauty Queen of Leenane[2]

I stop reading. And start again. I take in these few lines, the scarce words. And realise how much of the characters they allowed me to discover already.

Incredible.

My eyes keep scanning the text, back and forth, back and forth. I think this is it! I think I finally get what *'show rather than tell'* means!

* * *

When Luke sits down at my table, I ask him how he found the experience of writing the draft he sent me. He shakes his head, looks at me with a grimace, and sighs.

'Emma, what do all these authors mean when they keep saying "show rather than tell"? How do you do that? I tried but I really have no clue! I was trying to use my participants' words, and I thought that was going to "show"…but…I don't know…is that it?'

I look at the sagged shoulders, discomfited expression. I remember that feeling, during my PhD. Not being sure how to do what other scholars made seem easy, those harrowing words, 'show rather than tell', running in circle on my mind. Like a mantra. That's the moment I decide to try and show him, rather than tell him. I open the file of *The Beauty Queen of Leenane* on my laptop and turn it towards him, so he can read.

[*Five minutes later*]
I slowly take another sip of my mocha, then carefully place it back on the table. I feel as if I am trying to merge my body with the armchair, wanting to leave Luke time and space to read the text that was my 'Ah-ah' moment.

He lifts his eyes from the screen now, thoughtful.

'Ok…maybe I get it…I mean, I can see it here. I can see that the author is showing and not telling…but I am still not sure I get how I would do this.'

I nod, scroll up to the beginning of the scene, and point at the lines in front of us.

'Look at this scene. Maureen is wet, she is tired…both physically and mentally. She had to go out shopping, in the pouring rain, and now she is back and *"of course she is wet,"* how could she not be, with that rain?

But being home is not a relief for her – we know that immediately, when she sighs and just gets on with house duties. She has barely stepped into the room and taken her coat off, and her mother is already talking about herself and complaining to her. There is a weariness in the relationship between the two – can you see it? And the amount of demands that Mag places on Maureen is clear as soon as she says, "So you *can* get it yourself so" and "Well, can I help lumpy?". This short exchange also suggests the idea that there must have been a discussion before Maureen went out, something related to her mother asking her to get her Complan.'

Luke's eyes do not move from the screen, his face deep in thought, slowly nodding his head.

'How do we know all this?' – I continue – Because the author is *showing* all this information through the use of different techniques. First of all, the dialogue. But it is the *way* in which the dialogue is constructed that is telling. The short, dry exchange. The non-said, its implications, even louder than what is actually said.

Then we have the language register. "I did take *me* Complan." The grammar expression chosen takes us to a regional dimension, creates a background that goes beyond what has been described in the stage directions.

The stage directions themselves, though, help create the overall mood. Mag is described as "stoutish woman", who is "staring off into space" while on her rocking chair. Maureen, on the other hand, is "plain" and "slim" and constantly moving. She walks in from the outside, she is carrying bags, she takes her coat off, and starts setting the shopping away. There is a visual contrast created by these two characters, one almost still, the other in perpetual motion.

The contrast between the two characters is 'painted' immediately for the reader, even before there is any dialogue, and this is part of the 'showing rather than telling.' As soon as we hear the dialogue between the characters, we already know about the differences between the two, so we start interpreting their interaction as a consequence.'

'Ok – Luke says – so you are saying that "show rather than tell" is not just one technique, it is actually the result of using different techniques to get to this...I mean, when you read this scene it looks so simple, so stripped down of superfluous comments...but after listening to you, I can see that there is actually *a lot* going on behind! You said dialogue, the words chosen, the staging even...and the description of the characters...I mean, I didn't do that at all in my example. My character is only a voice...'

I am nodding vehemently; happy he is starting to see it.

'Yes, yes. Use of words, characters, dialogues...and even monologues, it does not always need to be a dialogue! Staging...and metaphors. They can be very powerful too.

What do you think, shall we try and tackle one technique at a time, see if that helps you?'

Layering

'Okay – says an eager Luke – how do I start though? I mean…how do I go from what I have here to what this should look like?'

'Well', I take another sip of my mocha, taking time to think how much I should tell him and how much I should let him discover, also through trial and error, 'first of all let's be clear: stories are not perfect or near detailed enough in the first writing instance or attempt. I wrote about eight different versions of my first creative nonfiction, before it felt at least good enough to share with others. One strategy I find useful is called *layering*. What do I mean by this? Well, when I commence the story writing process, I would do so by initially listing the characters involved. I then would list what each of the characters said, followed by the character's body language, the clothing they wore, the pitch of their voices, etc. I would then go back to the story and include other details, such as details of the surroundings, smells, and weather. To do this well, I have found that the story writing process involves a number of *layers* to ensure the picture (albeit made of words) is vivid enough so the reader can actually experience it as if they were there, and the words were showing them the intricate details of the encounter rather than me just telling them what was happening.'

Luke is scribbling down furiously on his notebook. He re-reads his notes and nods, satisfied.

'Well, looks like I need to go back and make a plan for this story. Think of my characters and start layering them then. I am starting to see all the things that are missing from my first draft!'

'Well, it is called a first draft for a reason. You know what my recommendation is, right?', a smile escaping across my face.

'Read some good examples!' Luke smiles back. 'Yes, it makes sense. I will do that and try to have a critical eye while reading, to notice all the techniques and aspects we mentioned!'

Choosing Your Words

[*One week later*]

PING! PING! PING! PING!

Aaargh! How can I have so many emails already? It's Monday morning!

I sift through my inbox…delete… delete… to read…to reply to…Oh! Luke! Let's see how he is doing with his story.

'Emma, I think I am starting to get it. I thought about our conversation the other day and I did as you suggested…I read more and more examples of creative nonfiction.

I really enjoy Andrew Sparkes' work, like that 'Fathers and sons: In bits and pieces'[3] you sent me! I have been carefully examining his work, page by page. I read them over and over and I wondered, what is he doing which is so different to what I am doing? I immersed myself in his stories, his words, for hours. Finally, it dawned on me that when I am reading Sparkes' stories, I feel like I am actually there. Through his words, he has painted me a picture that is so vivid I actually feel like I am part of his experience, part of his story and part of his world. His stories are written in such a way, that I can feel what is happening, I can see what is happening, and I can hear what is happening. All of my senses are alive. Then I realise, he is showing me what is happening as if I am actually there and I am the main character in his masterpiece. His words are leading the way for me as his story is played out vividly in my mind.

I gave it a go then, just with short bits…I attached them for you to have a look at…do you think I am on the right way?'

Curious, I hurry to open the attached file.

TELLING: *I stand on the scales and I weigh 73 kilograms. I am disappointed.*
SHOWING: *My feet carefully step onto the cold metal square platform. My eyes look down and my body is rigid, careful not to move as I might increase the number. The pin swings past the number 71, then 72, before it settles on 73. My heart drops and shoulders immediately slump.*
TELLING: *It is winter and as I walk along the pathway towards the pool, I become cold.*
SHOWING: *I carefully and purposefully place my feet along the pathway, fearful of slipping on the ice. At the entranceway, I am met by a wave of chlorine fumes and humid air which is such a contrast to the air outside.*
TELLING: *The coaches monitor my eating at dinner time.*
SHOWING: *As I bring a spoonful of rice to mouth, I feel their eyes gazing on me. They are sitting over the other side of the room, in their collared shirts, with their rotund bellies, with the cord of the stopwatch hanging out of their pocket. Their presence is so strong that it actually feels like they are sitting right beside me.*

'What's that sly smile?', comes Mike's voice from the desk next to mine.

'Just happy to see my student is starting to get what to do with his results…', I say, while my fingers are already tapping away a reply to Luke.

Metaphors

'Okay, let's talk about more ways to effectively "bring in" the reader. If I say *metaphor*, does it ring any bell?'

'Well, it definitely rings like school, GCSEs and all that...long time ago! Refresh my mind?', says Luke, grinning.

'It is a figure of speech that describes one thing in terms of something else, and it is extremely useful to communicate experiences in a vivid way, affecting how people feel, think, and behave.[4]'

'I see...I guess that by being so vivid and powerful, metaphors then help develop the story in a way that shows, rather than tell?'

'Exactly!'

'But how do I find the right metaphors? How do I know a certain expression is going to be effective?'

'Well, you know, it is not about becoming a poet all of a sudden. Metaphors are social creations, which are already present in our culture[5] – I look up to see Luke's blank expression – Ok, let's look at this from a practical perspective.'

I quickly find the file of my published creative nonfiction[6] and open it, then turn the screen towards Luke.

'Can you find all the metaphors I used in the story to describe pain?'

Luke starts skim-reading the paper. Every time he finds a metaphor, we write it down on the notebook next to us (Figure 1.1).

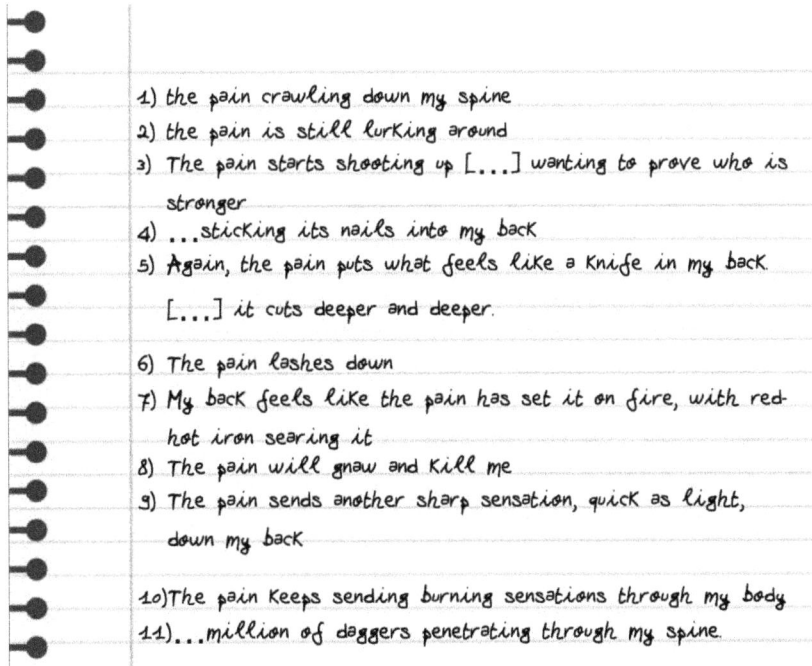

1) the pain crawling down my spine

2) the pain is still lurking around

3) The pain starts shooting up [...] wanting to prove who is stronger

4) ...sticking its nails into my back

5) Again, the pain puts what feels like a knife in my back. [...] it cuts deeper and deeper.

6) The pain lashes down

7) My back feels like the pain has set it on fire, with red-hot iron searing it

8) The pain will gnaw and kill me

9) The pain sends another sharp sensation, quick as light, down my back

10) The pain keeps sending burning sensations through my body

11) ...million of daggers penetrating through my spine.

Figure 1.1 Metaphors for pain.

Once he finishes, he is nodding, a focused gaze.

'Ok, I think I get what you mean by saying that metaphors are already in our culture. These images make sense...you made the pain look like an animal, sometimes a killer, but these expressions already exist in our imaginary.'

I smile, glad to see this little exercise worked.

'So, I guess now I need to think of what metaphors could help to represent the themes in my study. There is sadness for leaving the sport, which has been such an important part of my participants' lives. So maybe use images of something empty. And the anger towards bad leadership... I wonder how I could describe that? Oh, well, looks like I have something to reflect on while on the train! And then, shall I give the story another try?'

How Many Characters?

'Well done, Luke! Your story improved so much already! Great effort!'

Luke, sitting in front of me at the Uni café seems to grow taller with my compliments, but they are really well-deserved. His second draft is definitely something we can properly work on now.

'There are a few aspects I'd still like you to work on. I only have an hour before my next lecture, so this might be a bit full-on. You have your coffee? Ready to get going?'

'Just a sec, let me open a new file to take notes...I will try and do some work immediately after the meeting so that our conversation is fresh on my mind.'

Click, click, click...

'Ok, I am ready! And can I start with a question?' – I nod and wait – 'In your comment here, you said you got lost among the characters, that there should be fewer. But how do I choose who to keep, who to make speak?'

'Ha, that's a very good question. Let's start from there then.

You are right. Choosing your characters can be really tricky. When I was writing my creative nonfiction, I think my first draft had something like six characters. I had three gymnasts, two coaches, and one gymnast's mother. I had more than a year worth of data, among interviews, observations, focus groups, and informal conversations. Although I had the themes from my analysis to represent, it was still an overwhelming amount of information and I really felt like six characters was the *minimum* I could have to be able to represent all the themes. But not according to my supervisor. He kept "getting lost". I did wonder if at times he was doing it on purpose, to push me and see if I could make them fewer and fewer!'

'Well, you ended up with only two! How did you manage? How did you make sure you did not lose information?'

'Well, I think there were different processes that helped me at the time. You are right, I was extremely worried about not showing the themes, not representing my results effectively, and so I had different characters to make sure that through their dialogues all the different themes were discussed. I was also obsessed with using the exact same sentences they used, which somehow made it more difficult to merge characters.'

'Are you saying you had to choose between what to represent then?'

'No. Or at least, not in the sense you mean. I still represented all my themes, I just learnt to use different techniques to do that.'

Luke is now leaning forward, as if I am about to tell him the most profound secret ever. In the silence around us, I can feel him holding his breath, which makes me laugh. None of what I am about to tell him is a secret, neither is it my discovery. It is simply the experience of having used what others have written and talked about.

'Nothing extraordinary, Luke. Funny enough, these techniques are actually "very normal things," stuff we do every day, the whole time. I just learnt to use these when writing, being aware of the effect each technique could provoke.'

'Okay. Is this something else you want me to read about?'

'Haha, well, you know me enough, I think reading is always helpful. Some really good books I used when I was learning were Gutkind's "You can't make this stuff up"[7] and Pelias' "The Creative Qualitative Researcher."[8] But I'll start telling you something about these techniques. The main ones I have used to help decrease the number of characters without losing information I wanted to convey have been *dialogues* and *monologues*. These really linked with the idea of "voice." And then I think the overall *staging* of the story also helped me get across some important aspects.'

'Voice... dialogues... staging...,' Luke mutters under his breath while writing.

I take a sip of my coffee and get ready to examine the first of those techniques.

Choosing Your Voice: Narrative Perspectives and Interaction

'Let me start with a question: what made you decide to write the story in first person?'

Luke looks at me, eyes wide. 'Well... I am not sure...it just felt like the right way to do... I didn't really think about it. Is it wrong?'

'No, not at all. Writing in first person is often the most straightforward technique, because somehow it makes it easier to make the story compelling. The 'I' is feeling, thinking, acting, and everything is immediate, without filters,[9] so the reader is drawn in almost naturally.'

'Yes, I see what you mean. I guess I thought it was going to be the best way to achieve that show rather than tell…'

'…possibly. But then, if you think back to the first piece of reading that I gave you, the one we discussed in the café, that was using the voice – or the perspective – of a third-person narrator. One that is called all-knowing. When you choose to use that kind of perspective, or even a different third-person narrative, you are opening up different possibilities.'

'Ok,' – Luke looks blankly at the notebook in front of him – 'so what should I do? Who should tell the story?'

'Wait, I am not saying you need to change the voice. Just that you need to be aware of what each type of narrator allows you to do. There are so many variations, don't think of it only as first person versus third person. How do you think a first-person narrator can sound like?'

'Well…I guess here I used it in two ways… at the beginning of the story it helps me show how the character actually feels, the struggles, the doubts. But then at the end, in the last scene, he is sort of remembering, thinking back, reflecting…'

'Exactly, look at how many different aspects you were tackling without even being aware of doing that! You see, in the majority of your story, you achieve that subjectivity using lots of examples of *interior monologues*, which is a way of allowing the reader to peek into the character's thoughts and feelings. And at the end, that last scene you mentioned, could almost be considered an example of *detached autobiography*, where the 'I' reviews their choices with the power of hindsight, possibly sharing his learning with the other character, which could be the reader themselves…'

'Wow…I had never really thought of it that way…potentially talking to the reader…'

'Well, this would not be exactly like addressing the reader directly – what is called a *dramatic monologue* – but still, the reader might find themselves learning from your character's experience and so is your second character in that final scene.'

'What about what you did in your story?[10] You have two characters, but they both talk in first person… what voice would that be then?'

'That's a good question. That would still be first-person narration, but you see, for me it was very important to show that there wasn't a 'good cop/bad cop' situation, it was more nuanced than that. Using only a single first-person narrator in my case meant losing probably what I considered my most important finding from the research, the lack of communication. I felt using a monologue – so, first person – was more effective, but I needed to show the subjectivity of each character's experience. Which is why I decided to alternate first-person narrators, each with their own story, each with their own perspective of the same situation.'

'So many possibilities… and this is just writing in first person! I didn't realise how difficult choosing who is telling the story could be.'

'I am not sure if this helps but I once read in a lovely book, 'Reading like a writer'[11] – and something else…long title… – that the question that is really important and can help deciding on the point of view is not *who is telling the story*, but *who is listening?* And I think when we use storytelling to represent research, this is even more important.'

'Think of your audience...,' Luke is writing again in his notebook.

The queue at the café is long, the noise around us increasing, and my coffee is finished. All signs that I need to go and prepare the room for my lecture.

'I think you have enough information to chew on for a few days. I'll give you one piece of homework though: go to the bookshop around the corner, upstairs, first floor, where they have all the fiction. And just browse through the books there, look at the first page of a few novels, try to recognise the different voices, and see if that helps you or maybe inspires you in any way.'

Luke smiles, nodding away while throwing his notebook in the backpack. 'Around the corner, you said. Perfect!'

* * *

[Three days later]

Dear Emma,

Thank you so much for our meeting the other day, it was really useful. And the homework you gave me. Wow! It was so interesting! Suddenly I started noticing so many different things, just stuff I never paid attention to before when I was reading a novel. I ended up buying 4 books! Hahaha! They all have different types of narration and I was so curious after our conversation that I wanted to have more time to see how they developed. If you don't mind, below are some notes I took when reflecting on them, and then some more questions.

"Nutshell" by McEwan. Have you read it? It's crazy, it is written from the perspective of a fetus! I haven't really got into it yet, but I found it so interesting because it was so...well, not just subjective, somehow it seems to go beyond that. But then I kept thinking 'who is this story for?' and I can see its power.

I then got one for my sister, she is a feminist and the book was listed amongst feminist readings. "Women Talking," by Miriam Toews. It is based on a true story, so it made me think of research and creative nonfiction. That book is still written in first person, but at the same it feels much more detached, because it is more about this first person who describes everything through 'minutes of meetings'. Almost trying to

*give a quality of objectivity to something subjective.
I think maybe it could be an example of that 'dramatic
monologue' you mentioned the other day.*

*Another book I got for my sister – it's her birth-
day soon, so I thought first I'll use them for my dissertation, and then as a nice present – is called
"A Woman is No Man," by Etaf Rum. That is an example
of alternated first-person narrators, but there are at
least four different ones. Seems like it could become
confusing – I was thinking of our previous conversation on the amount of characters – but maybe in a
novel there is more time to develop each voice.*

*Finally, the one I actually started reading is "Nor-
mal People," by Rooney. Did you read it? I chose that
one because it uses a third-person narration, which
was the one we discussed the least the other day. One
thing I noticed is that whereas in first person you end
up writing monologues more easily, using third person
allows you to create dialogues. I find the story very
dynamic, maybe even more realistic?*

*It would be great to hear your thoughts on the use
of dialogues, because I am trying to add one in my
second scene, but I am struggling…should I just use
it to 'lighten up' all that thinking?*

Looking forward to hearing from you,

Luke

* * *

Hi Luke,

*Thank you for your email, it was great to see all
the work you are putting into this, and I really enjoyed reading your analysis of those different books.
I read the book by Etaf Rum, one of my favourite books
ever, it will be a great gift!*

*I also read "Normal People" – it was more than a
year ago, but I flicked through it again to see if I
could give you examples from it to answer your questions on the use of dialogues. First of all, when you
look at using third-person narration, you need to be
aware of three main strategies that can be used[12]:*

1   *Limited omniscience – the narrator only knows how
    one character feels and thinks, everything else is
    a surprise.*

2 *Omniscience – this is the all-knowing narrator I was telling you about.*
3 *Objective point of view – this perspective only allows the narrator to know what can be observed externally. Almost like a documentary.*

Rooney's novel uses the second point of view. The narrator knows everything, tells us about how Marianne and Cooper are feeling, what they are thinking, and so on. Even the way it is written, with no inverted commas to signal dialogue, I personally found it very interesting. It gives you an idea of this voice that is watching everything, already knows everything, and is just recounting what is happening, almost detached. At the same time the description, the dialogues, and the reaction of the characters provide a great depth.

Now, to answer your question about the use of dialogues, no, a dialogue can do much more than just 'lighten up' the story from all that insider perspective you were talking about. Dialogues are an extremely powerful instrument, when writing (non)fiction. As a technique, it extends our understanding of each character, and most importantly – especially when representing research – it allows you to portray complexity of findings. Different perspectives. Will Storr, in his 'The Science of Storytelling'[13] describes dialogue as 'dense with narrative information', and as an art. I love it when he says that dialogue,

> *can give us clues about everything we need to know about the character: who they are, what they want, where they're going, where they've been, their social background, their personality, their values, their sense of status, the tension between their true self and the false front they are presenting, their relationship to other characters, the secret torments that will drive the narrative forwards.*
>
> (pp. 133–134)

I'll try to give you a practical example. It is from a book I recently finished reading, "The Cleaner of Chartres" by Salley Vickers. The beginning of a chapter[14] saw the main character, Agnès, intent on working – and thinking – while her employer keeps talking to her. Look at how much narrative information is conveyed here:

'It is what Dylan Thomas based his *Under Milk Wood* on. You know Dylan Thomas?'

Agnès shook her head.

'Great English poet. Welsh, I should say. The Welsh would shoot me hearing me say that. I was nine, no, hang on, ten it must have been and my cousins Gwen and Gareth were with us there. The twins. They were my Aunty Mary's – my father's sister, she was a great knitter, Mary – G and G we called them, sometimes Gee Gee, which frankly they didn't like. I don't blame them, do you?'

Agnès said that she didn't.

'You know, I'm sure it didn't but in my memory it rained every day and we didn't mind because the rock pool were full of finds – winkles, anemones, goby fish. Shrimps of course. Plenty of those. Gwen was a demon shrimper. We boiled them up in a billycan on a primus stove. D'you like shrimps, Agnès?'

Agnès said that she did.

'Gareth, now, he wasn't such a keen shrimper. He wasn't as patient as his sister/ Boys aren't, you know. He and I got into trouble because we went into a cave and nearly got cut off by the tide. Our parents smacked us both. I remember it because we knew we had it coming and we vowed not to cry. I think I did. You could do things like that to children then.'

The professor's eyes indicated that he might be missing those far-off libertarian days.

'Where are they now?' Agnès asked.

'Who?'

'Your cousins.'

'Oh,' said the professor vaguely. 'I'm not sure. Gwen became a nurse, no, a physiotherapist. She worked with strokes, I seem to think. She must be retired now. I can't remember what happened to Gareth. An accountant maybe?' He frowned, unwilling to be hauled away from his lost idyll by the problematic present.

It is interesting how there is a dialogue, without really having a dialogue, at least until the end of the page. One character is talking, in quite a lot of detail and of personal memories. Agnès is working, and while we know she is answering, we don't 'see' her doing so, because her answers are just reported by the narrator, rather than voiced by her. What kind of information does this choice of formatting dialogue provide you with? And what happens at the end, when we finally 'hear' Agnès' voice? What changed? What is the author drawing attention to?

Well, I think I wrote enough. I will leave you pondering these questions, and shall we pencil one more meeting in our diaries to finalise your story, before the deadline for the dissertation submission? Let me know.

Best wishes,
Emma

* * *

[*One week later*]

'Well done, Luke! I loved reading the latest version of the story. That scene you included to show the stressors involved within the sport, I loved the rhythm of it and all those thoughts going on, the insight you are giving into the character, into your participants... Really, well done!'

'Aw, I am so glad you liked it, Emma. I wasn't sure if it was the best way to show that... I tried with a dialogue, and I did try changing voice and perspective, but in the end, this seemed to work better. Happy you think that too. Instead the last scene...it's not working yet. I know we need the dialogue, because of the aim of the scene, that portraying different perspectives... Yet, I cannot make it work.'

'Yes, I see your point. It is not at the level of the others. What is it that you are struggling with there?'

'Well, I guess it's the dialogue itself. I mean, the rest of the story is much more a monologue, I worked out how to represent my findings there. But here... how do I find a balance between the creative and the nonfiction in a dialogue? When I just copy quotes from the interviews in, they don't work, and I cannot figure out why.'

'Mmm. I see. Well, I don't think it's the fact that the quotes don't work as a conversation. I mean, you are representing your findings, it is important that the story is grounded in the data, so I agree that using quotes is fundamental. Yet, think of the book you were reading, "Normal People," think of those conversations, the way they were portrayed... what do they 'look' like?'

When Luke looks at me, I can almost see a big question mark forming above his head.

'Tricky question, I know, sorry. What I mean is that when you read dialogues in stories, they never look like dialogues in real life. When you conduct an interview and then transcribe it, how many "hmm" and "er" do you have? There are too many components of an everyday conversation that cannot be used when you are making characters talk on the page. Fictional dialogue cannot and should not sound like real speech; otherwise it becomes boring to read.[15] As a researcher, working on representing real data in a creative way then, this means you need to keep the core of your participants' quotes, but work to achieve economy, get to the point, as if you were creating a "smoother" version of a real-life conversation.'

I see Luke stiffening, a question on his lips, taking a moment too long to come out, while he ponders how not to offend me.

'Is it ethical to do so?', he asks.

'It would be unethical not to do so', I reply, quoting Bloom's words in her paper 'Living to tell the tale: The complicated ethics of creative nonfiction,'[16] and I continue explaining that,

> writers of creative nonfiction are dealing with versions of the truth, they – perhaps more consistently than writer in fictive genres – have a perennial ethical obligation to question authority, to look deep beneath the surface, and an aestethic obligation to render their versions of reality with sufficient power to compel readers' belief.

'You make a great point, Luke. We normally discuss how creative nonfiction is an ethical way of representing stories and experiences of sensitive topics through composite characters, highlighting our attention to our participants' privacy and confidentiality. Yet, we don't often discuss how we can be ethical towards the reader. What is the correct balance between the 'creation' and the 'nonfiction'?[17] Nonfiction writers discuss three 'lies' that are acceptable: little white lies used when memory blurred the details; lies demanded by the narrative structure, like composite characters, compression of time; and what's been called 'the gift of perhaps,' those conjectures in which a writer reveals what was not witnessed. See, your 'cleaning up' a quote does not make your representation unethical, it is just a matter of aesthetics, fundamental in a creative nonfiction.'

'Okay, I see. Thank you, that helps.'

'Good, I'm glad it does. Now, there is one more thing I'd like you to polish – let's say – before submission. It goes back to that layering technique we discussed a few weeks ago, and I think now that your story has been developed, you can focus on a few additional details, really nail the "frame", the setting of your story. Imagine this as a creative way to tease out nonfictional details. But before we move on, would you like a coffee? That conversation was quite intense.'

The Setting

I love the feeling I get wrapping my hands around a warm cup of coffee. My shoulders instantly relax, my mind resets. I take my time with a few sips, allowing Luke to tidy up his notes. A quick glance at my watch tells me I need to keep this short, or I'll lose his attention. We have been working for almost one hour.

'Okay, ready? This last bit is simpler – I think – than the rest, but it really gives you a chance to make things come together.'

'Of course,' Luke's usual eagerness takes over any signs of being tired, 'what is it?'

'It's the way you stage your story. And I am still talking about creative nonfiction, not theatre scripts and so on. It is the way you can use the setting of your story to reveal something about the characters, or their emotions, or even to add something to the plot.[18] For example, you could link people to places. The way we see a place is often related to how we feel in that moment. Think of how your character feels in the club bar after the match they won. Everyone is happy, drinking, enjoying themselves after the match. But for him, who has been secretly thinking of quitting, that game meant something else. The way he sees the bar is different, somehow darker. The armchair is in a corner, slightly hidden, he doesn't want to be seen by those he is struggling to relate to.'

Luke is writing down, but I want to make sure he gets this. I open my Mac and flick through some files.

'Look at this scene here.'[19]

> Sylvia: *(sighing)* I don't know...but we keep having lots of arguments, and since this back pain started it's just non-stop...it ruined the harmony in the family. *(staring into space)*
>
> Gym Mum 1: I know what you mean... Sunday lunch at Granny's and the nice long weekend walks are just a memory nowadays... if we are not in a gym hall, we are home studying and doing homework.
>
> *The waitress arrives with two big mugs, which she places in front of Sylvia and Gym Mum 1, and a small espresso cup for Gym Mum 2. Then she walks away.*
>
> Sylvia: And if that's not enough, Georgia keeps being in pain, and I cannot help but have that voice in the back of my head saying "Your mother is right, you should stop her"... *(Sylvia's head falls forwards, her shoulder slump)*
>
> Gym Mum 2: *(looks at Sylvia with a confused expression; in the meantime, she is putting the sweetener in the coffee and stirring with the teaspoon)*
>
> Sylvia, come on! You cannot be like this! Back pain is normal in gymnastics, everybody has it. I don't get nervous with Jade. [*mimicking talking to her daughter*] 'You have pain? Well, let's see...let's start with simple ways of taking care of it.' Then, when she can't take it anymore...for example if she can't train, because she can't jump, she can't do anything, and this has been going on for long, *then* I'll take her to the doctor.

'Now, this is not just a creative nonfiction, but what I wanted to show you was that idea of using the setting and using objects in ways that allow you to tell something about your character(s) without saying it.'

'Show rather than tell...'

'Exactly. That point where you have the waitress arriving with two big mugs of coffee, compared to the small, contained, somehow self-controlled espresso cup. The use of the sweetener, not sugar. That lack of understanding of pain in her daughter. These are all little details in the setting that are there to give an overall impression of this character, and highlight – without openly saying so – two different individuals, different perspectives, different ways of being.'

'I think I see what you mean. It's not just through dialogue or even voice choice that you can show differences...' Luke's eyes are sparkling, a smile spreading on his face. 'I think I know what details are missing. I need to rush now, I have a lecture, but I'll send you my final draft soon. Thank you so much for all your help!'

'My pleasure, Luke. I really hope it was useful. Good luck with your story!'.

Acknowledgements

I would like to thank Jenny McMahon and Camilla Knight for their invaluable and encouraging support with initial brainstorming and feedback on this chapter, and Andrew Wright for giving me permission to use excerpts from his initial dissertation drafts.

Notes

1 Some of the work presented in this chapter is taken from Mr Andrew Wright's undergraduate dissertation, 'Understanding dropout in Cricket,' with his consent.
2 McDonagh (2013).
3 Sparkes (2012).
4 Lakoff and Johnson (2008).
5 Gergen (1999).
6 Cavallerio et al. (2016).
7 Gutkind (2012).
8 Pelias (2019).
9 Anderson (2013).
10 Cavallerio et al. (2016).
11 Prose (2012).
12 Anderson (2013).
13 Storr (2020).
14 Vickers (2017, p. 80).
15 Prose (2012).
16 Bloom (2003, p. 278).
17 Bradley (2007).
18 Anderson (2013).
19 Cavallerio et al. (2021).

References

Anderson, L. (Ed.). (2013). *Creative writing: A workbook with readings.* Routledge.
Bloom, L. Z. (2003). Living to tell the tale: The complicated ethics of creative nonfiction. *College English, 65*(3), 276–289.

Bradley, W. (2007). The ethical exhibitionist's agenda: Honesty and fairness in creative nonfiction. *College English, 70*(2), 202–211.

Cavallerio, F., Wadey, R., & Wagstaff, C. R. (2016). Understanding overuse injuries in rhythmic gymnastics: A 12-month ethnographic study. *Psychology of Sport and Exercise, 25,* 100–109. https://doi.org/10.1016/j.psychsport.2016.05.002

Cavallerio, F., Wadey, R., & Wagstaff, C. R. (2021). Impacting and being impacted by overuse injuries: An ethnodrama of parents' experiences. *Qualitative Research in Sport, Exercise and Health.* https://doi.org/10.1080/21596 76X.2021.1885480

Gergen, K. J. (1999). *An invitation to social construction.* Sage.

Gutkind, L. (2012). *You can't make this stuff up: The complete guide to writing creative nonfiction—from memoir to literary journalism and everything in between.* Da Capo Lifelong Books.

Lakoff, G., & Johnson, M. (2008). *Metaphors we live by.* University of Chicago Press.

McDonagh, M. (2013). *The beauty queen of Leenane.* A&C Black.

McEwan, I. (2016). *Nutshell.* Vintage Publishing.

Pelias, R. J. (2019). *The creative qualitative researcher: Writing that makes readers want to read.* Routledge.

Prose, F. (2012). *Reading like a writer: A guide for people who love books and for those who want to write them.* Union Books.

Rooney, S. (2018). *Normal people.* Faber&Faber.

Rum, E. (2019). *A woman is no man.* HarperCollins.

Sparkes, A. C. (2012). Fathers and sons: In bits and pieces. *Qualitative Inquiry, 18*(2), 174–185. https://doi.org/10.1177/1077800411429095

Storr, W. (2020). *The science of storytelling: Why stories make us human and how to tell them better.* Abrams.

Toews, M. (2019). *Women talking.* Bloomsbury Publishing.

Vickers, S. (2017). *The cleaner of chartres.* Penguin.

2 From Telling to Showing

An Account of Developing a Creative Nonfiction

*Laura Martinelli, Melissa Day,
and Francesca Cavallerio*

Introduction

The aim of the chapter is to provide an account that outlines my (Laura's) process of moving from telling to showing the reader about themes. As such, the chapter describes, justifies, and demonstrates several methods, techniques, and collaborations that were central to the process of writing a creative nonfiction (CNF). Specifically, the challenges of converting raw data into themes, using themes to guide the construction of a first-person story, and transforming key elements of the story into imaginable scenarios that give the reader more opportunity to explore characters' relationships and emotions in the story. We hope this chapter elucidates the multiple stages and thorough work that is required to produce such qualitative products in a way that makes it achievable for others to experiment with.

How It Started: Using Holistic-Content Analysis to Develop Themes

My PhD, supervised by Melissa, was framed by narrative methodology and sought to explore coaches' vicarious experiences of injury in sport. I used Holistic-Content Analysis (Lieblich et al., 1998) to make sense of multiple semi-structured interviews with ten sport coaches of varying age, sport coaching experience and qualification who shared their experiences of witnessing injury in sport. The Holistic-Content Analysis (HCA) method initially required empathetic readings of the data to document initial and global impressions. These impressions were then discussed between Mel and I, and a decision was made about the "special foci of content or themes" (Lieblich et al., 1998, p. 63). Guilt was one of several special foci. From here, the analysis method involved coding and tracking "guilt" within individual stories, with relevant extracts being examined and clustered. This process led to a set of storied themes that addressed (a) the *development* of guilt, (b) the *regulation* of guilt, and (c) the *enduring effects* of guilt. The themes were labelled as

DOI: 10.4324/9781003038900-4

follows: "the inevitable and visceral nature of guilt"; "guilt-inducing thoughts about the injury"; "knowledge of and closeness with the injury athlete"; "establishing a contactable distance"; "seeking reparation through punishment"; "terminating oneself as a coach"; "learning from perceived mistakes." Results addressing the development and regulation of guilt were published (Martinelli et al., 2017) in a special issue of 'Sports Coaching Review' on the emotional demands of coaching. An overview of the results addressing the enduring effects of guilt was later provided in a book chapter (Martinelli & Day, 2020).

Having taken a *story analyst* position (Smith & Sparkes, 2009) and in choosing a realist tale form of representation in our published journal article (i.e., Martinelli et al., 2017), I presented and scrutinised snippets of the coaches' stories to demonstrate themes and theory. This meant the results section 'chopped and changed' between different individual stories, as I took the reader on a highly guided tour and interpretation of 'things' that generated, exacerbated, or regulated a subjective state of guilt for sport coaches in the context of an athlete's injury. This gave the reader little opportunity to make sense of the coaches' stories as they see fit. Furthermore, although I had given examples of the ways the coach's knowledge of, and closeness with, the injured athlete had a meaningful impact on the guilt experienced, I felt results were limited in showing two aspects: the way the coach-athlete relationship foregrounded the coaches' experience of athletes' injuries, and what the injury had meant for the coach-athlete relationship.

Revisiting the Data: Placing a Spotlight on the Portrayal of Characters

As a narrative researcher, I was fascinated by the portrayal of the injured athlete: the way the coaches characterised their injured athletes in different ways, what this characterisation inferred about their relationship with the athlete, and how it shaped and provided a backdrop to their experience of the injury and a subjective state of guilt – felt by coaches or interpreted by myself. I decided to re-immerse myself in the raw data for the purpose of exclusively understanding the portrayal of the injured athlete. I stayed within my comfort zone, using holistic content techniques to help me conclude a series of characterisations that were pertinent to the coaches' stories of the emotional impact of an athlete's injury. Whilst I was conscious that this approach was still reducing the relational element of the coaches' stories to a set of factors, it helped me to confidently identify a coach ("Andrew"), whose interviews were in abundance of talk about his knowledge of, and degree of closeness with, an injured athlete and who used such talk to set the scene or to justify his experience of the injury.

Conducting Narrative Analysis to Create a First-Person Story

According to Polkinghorne (1995) narrative researchers may conduct interviews with participants in ways that do not produce ready-made stories, but instead offer up scenes, characters, and plots in a fragmented form. This was my experience of the interview data generated with Andrew. In such cases, Polkinghorne (1995) details a Narrative Analysis method that searches for, filters, and amalgamates relevant data in a way that moves from isolated and seemingly unrelated elements to a meaningful whole with explanatory power. The final product of this analysis method is a first-person story that provides a coherent, developmental account and plausible explanation of the culmination of a final outcome.

As part of my Narrative Analysis, I searched for relevant interview extracts regarding the characterisation themes (see previous section). Furthermore, data regarding the coach's early experiences of the athlete, their experience of the athlete's injury, attempts to regulate guilt, and an indication of the current status of the relationship was also extracted. Extracts were then chronologically grouped and ordered to achieve a temporal flow. Next, 'narrative smoothing' (i.e., small adjustments to grammar and punctuation of sentences, to enhance the clarity of the meanings narrated while keeping close to the participant's unique use of language; Polkinghorne, 1995, p. 16) was performed. Once an initial draft had been composed, it was read by various audiences, including family and friends, a small group of undergraduate students, and Mel for feedback. A final draft of the first-person story was created and sent to sport coaches and sport psychology practitioners, asking them what the story made them think and feel. Their responses were reported within my PhD to demonstrate the value of this form of qualitative research, to exemplify the different ways that others may respond, and to consider the implications of these responses for the narrator of such stories (see also Perrier et al., 2015; Soundy et al., 2010).

Moving Beyond What Was Said: Revising the CNF

Following responses to the story, I was aware it had the potential to provoke thoughts and feelings. When Fran invited me to contribute to this book presenting a CNF version of previous published work, I knew this was an opportunity to strengthen the potential of Andrew's story. Since my acceptance, there have been many texts, emails, and videocalls working through the process of transforming the first-person story in a way that does more to *show* rather than *tell*. The sections below present some example paragraphs from the original first-person story based on interview data with Andrew. Each paragraph is followed by an indication of feedback from Fran and my reflections and actions. This chapter ends with the revised CNF.

Example Paragraph 1: The Introduction to the Story and Characters

Andrew is a retired alpine ski coach, qualified to BASI level 3 standard. He has 33 years of coaching experience, some of which has been at a national and international level of competition. The following text represents Andrew's story of an injured athlete called Claude. It is narrated by Andrew:

> Claude was introduced to skiing by his wife, Aimee, after his motorbike accident when he was twenty-one years old. He lost the leg and his eye. Aimee wanted Claude to do something, so she encouraged him to go to the local ski slope and learn to ski. Sliced bread, the best thing, he loved it and it became his life, with any spare money being spent on new equipment. Claude came to me some years later as a result of a training camp that I had been coaching at. I thought he was a good skier. Very quiet. Bit reserved. I suppose my first impression of him was that he was a loner because he didn't say very much, he just sat in the back and he did what was asked. He'd be one of the first on the ski slope in the morning and then once training had finished, he'd carry on afterwards. He always wanted to do that bit more and could never see that less was better in some cases, so I was intrigued. It wasn't until the end of that camp that he asked me to be his coach.

FRAN: Can we re-think how we introduce the reader to this story? Maybe Andrew is an invited speaker at a coaching conference, and we first have him make some key recollections to someone that help us learn about Andrew? Also, can you have Andrew recall in more detail the moment that he first met Claude? Set this scene up so that it portrays Claude as quiet, a loner and of a reserved disposition etc. without explicitly telling the reader so.

LAURA: What was my impression of Andrew and how can I draw upon my experience and knowledge of him to create a fictitious scenario for the purpose of introducing him to the reader? It's been 8 years since I interviewed him! I know I made reflective notes after each interview and that Mel and I used to meet up regularly during data collection to help me reflect/debrief... [searches computer, finds a folder "Andrew Reflection". I start reading my notes and the memories of my first encounters with Andrew come flooding back]. Thank goodness I made those reflective notes!

Example Paragraph 2: Intentionally Changing the Tense

> Claude's got very strong will power and he's a very determined person; doesn't take no for an answer. He just threw himself down the

course during training, attacking everything as though his life depends on it and I'm saying "Claude, you don't have to ski like that. You only ski like that when it matters in a race." Claude believed in what we were doing together, I assume primarily because it gave him more success and satisfaction, and a sense of purpose. This did mean that Aimee, his wife, was put to one side, not nastily, but everything went down the route for skiing; it was his whole life really. He worked so that he could buy more equipment to ski. He didn't want to buy a new house or get a bigger house; he wanted to be able to have next year's skis because it might get him to the winning post. You wouldn't believe how competitive he was and still is.

FRAN: The tense of some of the sentences in this paragraph seems a bit weird – it's moving from present to past, to present again

LAURA: This was something that we noted when constructing the first-person story – it was how Andrew spoke. For me, it suggested that the relationship was not yet in the past despite not coaching the athlete for several years. Andrew said he still had contact and would meet up with Claude, so maybe that's also why he kept changing tense when talking about what Claude was or is like?

FRAN: This is interesting…I wonder if we can use the guest talk scenario to highlight this.

Example Paragraph 3: Slow Things Down, Create Suspension

It was six months after he made it into the top ten ranking when the incident happened. It was a bad break to his leg, three broken bones in total. At the time of the incident we were taking part in a training camp abroad, and I was acting as an assistant to the head coach, a guy called Simon. The slope we'd been allocated was like a sheet of ice. So I am trying to set up the giant slalom course on it with equipment that wasn't great, but it was the best that we could afford at a time when disabled sport had very little funding. I was having such trouble drilling the slalom poles into the ground. I couldn't get the rigid part on a couple of the poles underground so I raised my concerns with the head coach, who then gave the skiers clear instructions not to ski so close to the poles as they would usually do. Well, for Claude that was like a red rag to a bull because that's what he's trying to do – he's trying to get closer to the poles because it affects his line and how fast he's going. Claude caught his boot on one of the dodgy poles and hit the deck.

FRAN: Could this be expanded on, maybe slowed down, having some dialogues or even just thoughts in the coach's head while trying to drill the poles… and then contrasting with the following paragraphs, showing how quickly everybody moved and got into action. Having people shouting instructions, rather than saying what they did?

LAURA: But what would Andrew think of me embellishing his story like this? Although... it's not just Andrew's story anymore, it's also my story; it's just as much my story as it is Andrew's. Why do I still default to a post-positivist position? Maybe I should go back to those key readings on this, like Elliott (2005) and Josselson (2011).

The Revised Creative Nonfiction: Injury Was a Wake-up Call

"Mr Allsopp?

"Yes"

"I am Sarah from the organising committee [Smiles as she stands up from behind the welcome table that has a handful of name badges that have not yet been collected]. I hope you found us okay, we are so pleased to have you share your experience of injury, I think it's going to be a popular session [smiles again]. Your talk doesn't start for another hou__"

"I know" *Do I look that stupid* "Where am I doing it then?"

"You'll be in the Mitre Lecture Theatre. It's in a different building. I can take you across now unless you would like to have a walk around the campus or maybe get a drink first"

"Yes, I will have a coffee, with milk and two sugars please"

"Um, yes of course I can get that for you, refreshments are just this way"

[Sarah leads Andrew into the university canteen. He walks to a dining table while Sarah heads over to the drinks area. She operates the coffee machine, making two drinks, and then walks over to where Andrew has sat down].

"Is that okay?" [Sarah hands Andrew the drink]

"The head of department I once worked at used to say if it doesn't look like a cup of mud you haven't done it right"

"Do you want less milk, it's no problem"

"No, it will do"

[Andrew nods his head at Sarah as if to gesture for her to sit down. Sarah complies]

"You said head of department? Was that_"

"Is that not what you call them anymore. It was always the woodwork department when I taught"

"You were a schoolteacher?"

"Yes, that's how I got into ski coaching. Back in the late 60s we had a local residential centre open a dry ski slope and, because I was a teacher, I had access to it, mostly a case of being self-taught. There was a group of us across the county meeting up, developing our own take on dry slope skiing and how to teach it. Then a couple years later, a guy called Robert came along who was a proper skier, he ran a few sessions, linked us up with a few courses in the Alps. For 20 years I was involved in the running and delivering of national courses where we trained and assessed other teachers so that they were competent enough to take pupils on ski residentials to the Alps. By the time I myself left teaching in school, I had arranged something like 40–50 school ski trips" [Andrew takes a large gulp of his coffee] *She looks interested, this is nice.*

"Wow, and then you started properly coaching after that?"

"No. [takes another gulp of coffee] ... It depends what you mean by coaching. If you want to know when I started offering coaching services, I was doing that at the weekend at the local dry slope alongside all the teacher training stuff, mostly teenagers, but there were a couple of disabled people. It wasn't like it is today where you have a proper qualification for coaching disabled skiers, we adapted and adjusted our coaching as we went along, we experimented with things as we learnt more about these disabled men or women that came along. [Sarah's phone starts ringing] It wasn't until around 2000 that I made the move to coaching disabled people and_"

"I am so sorry" [looks down at phone] "it's Jane, the conference chair, I really must answer it."

"Go ahead."

[60 minutes later, Andrew is stood at the front of the lecture theatre, he's just finished telling the audience about how he got into coaching in disability skiing]

"I've had ... I *had* the privilege of working as a ski coach for 33 years, a fulfilling career but I'm afraid that injury has very much been a part of it in a number of ways" *If they don't like hearing about injury, coaching probably isn't for them.*

"The last proper injury incident that I was involved in was Claude's. It was a bad leg break, three broken bones, and I thought it would be helpful to share with you a few things that happened leading up to that injury."

[Andrew looks around the room] *They really are a young bunch. Will they understand what I'm about to tell them, will they get it?* [takes a sip of water]

"Before I talk about the injury, let me tell you about Claude. He was introduced to skiing by his wife, Aimee, after his motorbike accident when he was twenty-one years old. He lost a leg and his eye. Aimee wanted Claude to do something, so she encouraged him to go to the local ski slope and learn to ski. Sliced bread, the best thing, he loved it. Any spare money went on new equipment. Skiing became his life."

[Andrew smiles, absent-mindedly]

"The first time I saw him properly skiing down a slalom course, he was throwing himself down mountain, attacking everything as though his life depended on it. Just as soon as he had entered the mid-section, he was out of there, poles still waving around like bobo dolls.

I can still picture him, getting to the bottom of the course, stopping within a few feet of me, and taking his helmet off, looking at me – I suppose for some sort of feedback. My mouth would have been hanging half-open if I wasn't trying to cover up my feelings. In my head I was saying 'what the bloody hell was that? Are we at a training day or have I missed the memo that this is some sort of qualifier event?', but I think I actually said, 'Can we just take it down a notch please and work on X or Y.'

You see my point? [Andrew scans the faces in the room] *hmm not sure, but they still look interested.* There was never any need to have those big conversations to motivate or ask for more from Claude; not like some poor coaches have to do with their athletes. Yeah, yeah, I can see a few of you nodding away. Jealous, aren't you? [Andrew smirks]

By the time I had figured out Claude, let me tell you, eventually those conversations turned into 'If you go back up that slope, then dinner is on you. You need to have a rest.' [Andrew looks and leans towards a group of people sitting in the front rows near to him] …I tell you, a lot of dinners ended up being on him." [the group of people laughs] *Those were good times…I can still hear Claude mumbling away that I was robbing him of money that he was planning on using to buy those new skis.*

"Claude even earned himself the nickname 'doghouse' for things like skimping on his wife's birthday present or using it as an excuse to take her skiing somewhere he wanted to try out. Never interested in a new car or paying for work they needed done on the house. It was always about getting the skis that would get him to the winning post.

He intrigued me. I can still see him in the de-briefing meeting after that first training session, sat in the second row from the front, just over to left. As the other skiers started to come in, they sat in the rows behind. Claude didn't even look up to see who was coming in." *I guess I liked that about him: quiet, reserved, just focused on doing what had been asked of him, not interested in the small talk.* "And then the next morning Claude was there at the bottom of the slope ready to get going. Later on that day I overheard Claude correcting the head coach about what time it was going to get dark, I presume he did that so he could have one more go down before training had finished. He always wanted to do that bit more.

So, what do you reckon? He sounds like the dream athlete, doesn't he? [Andrew looks at the audience] I can see some of you are hesitant to agree. Good. A word of caution to those of you who did nod: sometimes you will have athletes like Claude who will never see that less is better in some cases, and those are the ones that you need to … keep a close eye on."

[Andrew scans the room, pausing]

"At the end of the week, Claude found me in the bar one evening. No small talk, just came straight up to me and said, 'will you be my coach?'"

***

"why'd you want me as a coach?"
"well, I like your style, it suits me"
"you must think I'm a nutter, why would I want to take you on"
"because I want to improve"
"where do you want to be in 3 months? Where do you want to be in 6 months, in a year's time, in 20 years' time?"
"I don't know. That's why I need you to be my coach."

***

"From that point onwards, we spent a lot of time together driving to the Alps and from ski resort to ski resort, eating together most evenings. He always drank cokes or oranges, and sometimes looked down his nose at me because I would have wine with the meal. *Something to do with his childhood.* He's a self-reliant figure. There were countless times when we'd be getting on a ski lift. The lifty's reactions were a sight; eyes jittering about the place while they'd try to grab at Claude's arms to help him on but only ever making things worse. It would usually end with Claude pushing them away and by the time the lifty had scrambled back to his feet we'd be up on the lift laughing back at the gawping idiot."

***

"did you see the face of the lifty? Who did he think I was? Trying to help me like that, as if I needed help. I'm a man. Like my first coach, Michele, used to say: 'real men don't eat quiche'"

***

[Andrew's eyes are lost in memories for a second. He smiles to himself, and with a shrug of his shoulders he continues addressing the audience…]

"I was only starting to get to know him back then and learning about how he had been coached by others. I was taken back by some of the stuff he told me about his first ski coach, Michele. I remember saying to him, 'so tell me about a normal training session with Michele' and Claude, 'we would start by walking or pulling ourselves up the slope. No way would we dare drinking water, he'd call us a sissy for the rest of the session. Men need to be tough!' I remember nodding, realising the sort of coaching Claude was used to before me. All about grit. Old school, I guess we'd say.

What I am trying to say is that you have got to put that time and understanding in with your athletes, you have to know their back story, if you really want to help them excel. It's of no coincidence that within a year working together, he got to be tenth in the world. I will never forget the feeling you get seeing his name go up and up in the rankings, it's like my body and heart just has this extra buzz to it; like when a teacher tells you that your kid did something excellent at school that day. I saw beyond what others just thought of as quiet, reserved. To me he was the Superman or Spiderman of the ski world. It may sound ridiculous and up here, in my head, I knew it's a dangerous sport… but he is so… he was so good. He became something different to what I'd seen before. The best skier I'll ever know."

If only this is where the story could finish [Andrew clears his throat, takes a sip of water. A shaky hand places the glass back on the table]

"He had been in the top ten ranking for six months. We were at a training camp abroad and I was acting as an assistant to the head coach, a guy called Simon. The slope we'd been allocated was like a sheet of ice. I had been ordered to set up a giant slalom course. You could not imagine the equipment we had back then, when disabled sport had very little funding. Drilling the poles into the ground was a nightmare. I couldn't get the rigid part on a couple of the poles underground. I remember radioing Simon and losing it with him but all I got back was the muffled sound of Simon telling the skiers, 'some of the poles are dodgy so don't ski too close' [Andrew's head drops slightly, recalling more of that conversation].

***

'Simon, this is a fucking joke, too many of the poles won't fix in right, I'm telling you, we need to wait another hour for things to warm'
'Thanks Andrew, like I said, it's noted.'
'What the bloody hell does that mean? Simon? Can you hear me?"

***

I should have fought harder, protested further. But – you know – I'd ruffled enough feathers in the past lobbying about equipment issues... I could do with one less enemy. But I should have known better... I should have known Claude. Athletes like him, telling him not to ski close to the poles, it's like red rag to a bull. The closer to the pole, the better his line, the faster his time.

[Andrew looks at the young faces in the crowd] *Is there a chance that they can understand? What qualification level is this? Can't remember... early one though. They are keen, look at them. They do things by the book. Is this story going to help them or not?*
[there is a heavy silence in the room]

An hour later I was back at the bottom, a couple of guys who had done their course and were hanging around to see Claude come down. Then Claude appears on the horizon.
I looked up, and I knew it.
        I saw it before it happened.
            He was heading fast towards the pole,
                One of the dodgy ones I had struggled with.
Too fast.
Too close.
His boot caught on the pole and hit the deck. I saw and heard it all.

Almost before he was down, we got into action. Automatic pilot on, no time for thinking.
I rush down to the nearest ski lift, tell the lifty to call for the mountain rescue guys. They take Claude down in the wagon, and I am there at the on-piste medical site when they arrive. They rush Claude in, no time to waste, he has to be seen by the doctor. I can still hear his screaming, the agony when they are trying to take the boot off. Pure torture. 'Bad leg break, three broken bones', one of the rescuers tells me, seeing me sitting on the chair outside the room, a glove squeezed in my hands.
Before I know it, he's being transferred to the main hospital. They operate on him within 24 hours, put a titanium plate in with fourteen screws to hold all of the bits together.

[Pause. Silence. Andrew's knuckles white against the border of the table he has been leaning up against]

"That was a hell of a wake-up call... It was a bad break, and the surgeons did a fantastic job but with an injury like that there is a chance that it's not going to heal.
What if they have to amputate his only leg?
What will he do with himself if he doesn't have skiing?

How's he going to support himself and his family in a wheelchair?"

Why is my voice cracking? This was years ago, Andrew. Get. A. Grip. [Roaming the room, Andrew's eyes fall on the face of a young coach who is frowning] *Why are they frowning? Are they* interested or confused? *Or disappointed? Am I making sense? They need to know the whole story, then they will get it.*

[Andrew continues, focused on this one person in the audience]

"You see, prior to the accident, I didn't associate Claude with being in a wheelchair and for me the injury was like a 'bloody-hell-what-were-you-doing' moment. In my mind, Claude was Superman. How was this possible? He was invincible.

Yes, of course, I knew he wasn't, but it was as if my psyche had put it to one side, so when it happened, I thought 'why on earth have I been encouraging him to race?!' Why hadn't I thought he could ever hurt himself? Why? How stupid was that?

I didn't think that he could make a mistake and suffer a severe accident. 'Why not?', you might wonder. Well, knowing his background I guess I just felt he had already been through so much and had enough steel inside of him, that he was protected. But he was no Superman.

I should have known. We should have avoided it."

[silence]

"Does that make sense?

Like I said at the start, if you have a question or want me to explain something again, please ask"

[In the stillness of the room, a hand is slowly raised.]

"Yes?"

"It sounds like you are blaming yourself, but you were only the assistant coach. Shouldn't it be on this Simon guy?"

I wish. I wish it was.

"I was a part of the decision to allow Claude to go down that slope with those dodgy poles. I may have been the assistant coach that day, but I was still Claude's coach, you don't just clock on and off of your responsibilities as a coach. At a practical level, I should have insisted on speaking to Claude one-on-one before they sent the skiers up the lift. In that way, I am just as culpable as the head coach. What we did was wrong."[another hand goes up]

"Yes"

"Sorry if this is a stupid question but I am just wondering, what is a coach supposed to do if they think they've have done something wrong, something

that could have been avoided that has led to an athlete's injury? What are the rules?"

"Great questions. Rules change all the time, so I would prefer to speak about what it is that you as a coach think and feel you should do in those situations. For me, all I could think was that I had to help Claude somehow, so my reaction was to tell Claude to sue me."

***

"sue me, and the head coach"
"no way, I can't!"
"you've got to, it won't cost me, I swear. I'm insured for third party claims."

***

"Trying to get Claude to sue me went on for about a year. It may sound odd to you, but I couldn't stop thinking of ways to get Claude to come around to the idea of suing me. I would wake up and think, 'maybe today is the day Claude will change his mind and agree that we did him wrong.'"

"But wouldn't that have been a problem for you, had Claude sued you?"

"Yes, it would have. But it was the right thing to do, and I needed Claude to know that there was no expiry date on it."

[Another hand goes up. Andrew nods. A voice speaks]

"How did Claude respond to the injury?"

"Claude was being Claude. Right from the off he was saying 'oh, it will be alright.' In his mind it was a fait accompli: his leg would heal. 'It's only broken bone and it'll be stronger than it was before.' And me, saying to him, 'let's wait and see how it heals', thinking it may not heal. Claude was determined he was going to race again, his leg did heal, and so for the next couple of years we worked towards his comeback."

"You don't sound happy…?"

"You are right. I wasn't.

Not entirely.

I would have liked Claude to think about the bigger picture, to stop and consider what could have been if his leg hadn't healed. I kept hoping he'd tell me he was ready to change down a gear on the competition circuit, or maybe even take some time out to reassess. But Claude was being Claude."

"…so, you stayed? You coached him?"

"Sorry I didn't see where that question came from" [A hand belonging to an older male delegate, possibly late-30s goes up in the 5th row, Andrew makes eye contact him] "It's like in snooker, you know? You don't give up the frame when your opponent's at the table, there's a certain etiquette… and that's what I felt. Wrong? Maybe. I know other people would have just said 'no', boom, and they're off coaching the next athlete with potential."

[Andrew takes a sip of water]

"I stayed, because Claude had to try and see his way through to racing again. And because he told me, 'I need to do this, and I can't do it without you.' What could I have done? I owed him that. It was my job to be there for him and check he was more conscious of the dangers."

Conscious of the dangers! As if! I can still recall that sinking feeling in the pit of my belly, every time I saw him come over the horizon of a slope. The tightening around my neck, breathing impossible until he reached the bottom…

"…so did you coach Claude until you retired?"

Here we go. Let's get this over with, Andy. Get it out and go home.

"Well, his training was going quite well, on our way back to peak fitness and what we thought would be a Paralympic position… then they pulled the plug on Claude. To cut a long story short, when the injury happened, we should have logged the points Claude had accrued. There was… I guess there might still be… a protocol in place if a skier gets injured so that their status quo would still be recognised two years down the line."

Stupid protocol… no one told us…

"So yes, there was a protocol, but for the protocol to work, you have to fill out the right paperwork. If you don't, the skier's points lapse after a year.

Yes, you are guessing right.

We hadn't filled in the right paperwork.

Goodbye Paralympics."

[the room is silent]

"After that, things faded away. It was a difficult decision to stop coaching Claude. I knew it would affect him and his life. It wasn't going to be easy for him, but I had to do it. I had to. He was putting himself under extreme pressure. It was a decision I had to make for myself, but I knew that it would impinge on his situation.

Deep down he knew what I was thinking. We didn't need to speak about things and I didn't want it to be a sudden, 'I am no longer coaching you.' We'd come to it over time. I felt we… he… needed to look at life after skiing. I would just keep dropping it into conversations, every now and again. Things like 'Just imagine if you put this energy into coaching others, you'd be at the top of that game before you know it' or 'I've seen that you could be eligible for a paid position of a coaching course that's taking place in your favourite resort,' and so on.

Claude would just roll his eyes at me.

Slowly, I also started not being able to make things more and more. More often than not I'm saying to him, 'Sorry, no I can't do that, I've got so much on.'

He got the message, in the end. I told myself he could go to another coach.

I remember telling him, the writing's on the wall Claude and I can see it. Why fight a losing battle?"

"...so that's it, that's how it ended between you and Claude?", asks the frowning delegate.

"That's it."

Reflective Questions

1   What kind of feedback would you have given on the example paragraphs from the original first-person story?
2   How could the revised CNF be improved further? Are there any further changes you would suggest?
3   Thinking back to the list of themes that were generated via holistic content analysis techniques about the development, regulation, and enduring effects of guilt, how well does the revised CNF explore or represent these?

References

Elliott, J. (2005). Interpreting people's stories: Narrative approaches to the analysis of qualitative data. In J. Elliott (Ed.), *Using narrative in social research* (pp. 36–59). Sage. https://www.doi.org/10.4135/9780857020246

Josselson, R. (2011). "Bet you think this song is about you": Whose narrative is it in narrative research? *Narrative Works, 1*(1), 33–51.

Lieblich, A., Tuval-Mashiach, R., & Zilber, T. (1998). *Narrative research: Reading, analysis, and interpretation*. Sage.

Martinelli, L., & Day, M. (2020). Guilt experienced by coaches following athlete injury. In R. Wadey (Ed.), *Sport injury psychology: Cultural, relational, methodological, and applied considerations* (pp. 120–141). Routledge.

Martinelli, L. A., Day, M. C., & Lowry, R. (2017). Sport coaches' experiences of athlete injury: The development and regulation of guilt. *Sports Coaching Review, 6*(2), 162–178. https://doi.org/10.1080/21640629.2016.1195550

Perrier, M. J., Smith, B. M., & Latimer-Cheung, A. E. (2015). Stories that move? Peer athlete mentors' responses to mentee disability and sport narratives. *Psychology of Sport and Exercise, 18*, 60–67. https://doi.org/10.1016/j.psychsport.2015.01.004

Polkinghorne, D. E. (1995). Narrative configuration in qualitative analysis. *International Journal of Qualitative Studies in Education, 8*(1), 5–23. https://doi.org/10.1080/0951839950080103

Smith, B., & Sparkes, A. C. (2009). Narrative analysis and sport and exercise psychology: Understanding lives in diverse ways. *Psychology of Sport and Exercise, 10*(2), 279–288. https://doi.org/10.1016/j.psychsport.2008.07.012

Soundy, A., Smith, B., Cressy, F., & Webb, L. (2010). The experience of spinal cord injury: Using Frank's narrative types to enhance physiotherapy undergraduates' understanding. *Physiotherapy, 96*(1), 52–58. https://doi.org/10.1016/j.physio.2009.06.001

Part II

From Realist Tales to Creative Nonfiction

3 The Daily Grind

Being a Parent of a Competitive Junior Tennis Player

Camilla J. Knight and Chris G. Harwood

Introduction

Throughout a child's sporting life, many individuals impact upon their engagement and experience (Wylleman & Rosier, 2016). However, it is parents who usually have the most enduring impact (Knight, Berrow, & Harwood, 2017). For instance, research has shown that when children first start to participate in sport, it is parents who identify the opportunities, pay for sessions, and act as the taxi service taking children to and from training. As children progress, parents usually continue to fund engagement while also increasingly committing time and emotional energy to competitions and training. Subsequently, even as children head towards adulthood, parents continue to remain a crucial source of emotional and tangible support (Côté, 1999; Fredricks & Eccles, 2004; Harwood & Knight, 2015). However, fulfilling these roles, and providing this support to their children, is not always easy for parents. In fact, an ever-growing body of literature points to an extensive range of challenges and stressors that parents may encounter while attempting to facilitate their child's sporting involvement (Burgess, Knight, & Mellalieu, 2016; Harwood, Drew, & Knight, 2010; Harwood & Knight, 2009a, 2009b; Harwood et al., 2019; Hayward, Knight, & Mellalieu, 2017; Leinhart, Nicaise, Knight, & Guillet-Descas, 2020). These, in turn, can impact both the quality of children's sporting experiences and the lives of parents (Knight et al., 2017), as will become apparent throughout the current chapter.

The story that unfolds in this chapter is based upon two studies (Harwood & Knight, 2009a, 2009b) that I (Camilla) had the great pleasure of conducting for my undergraduate dissertation in 2005/2006, supervised by Chris. As a neophyte researcher and former competitive tennis player, I was excited to have the opportunity to engage with the parents of tennis players to learn about their experiences, particularly the stressors they encountered in supporting their children's tennis. I knew my own story, and thought I had an idea of what it had been like for my parents, but I wanted to know if it had been similar for others. In approaching these

DOI: 10.4324/9781003038900-6

studies, I hoped to collect some interesting data to give a voice to parents, something that was generally missing from the sport psychology literature at the time. I had an idea of the types of things parents might mention, such as time, travel, the commitment required, and finance (e.g., Baxter-Jones et al., 2003; Kirk et al., 1997a, 1997b, Wolfenden & Holt, 2005). But I wasn't prepared for the emotion they would share.

In study 1, the parents of 123 tennis players completed an extensive open-ended survey (Harwood & Knight, 2009a) and subsequently through study 2, a further 22 parents took part in face-to-face interviews (Harwood & Knight, 2009b) focused on understanding the stressors associated with parenting junior tennis players. As soon as we started to receive the completed surveys, I realised we had stumbled across a topic that really needed exploring. Parents' frustration, anger, worry, concern, and disappointment leaked from the pages; their sense of hopelessness, helplessness, and being overwhelmed shone through every interview. Streams of information were shared, with parents writing up the sides of the survey, on blank pages, and even attaching additional sheets to ensure they could fully share their experiences. Capital letters, multiple underlining of words, and exclamation marks adorned the survey pages, while tears, exhausted laughter, head shaking, and periods of quiet reflection punctuated the interviews. I left each interview exhausted, desperate to call my parents to apologise for what they must have gone through supporting me as a junior player.

I transcribed the surveys and the interviews and fully immersed myself in the data. I read and re-read the information that had been shared over and over again. I dreamt about the data, I knew the narratives by heart, I could quote the data verbatim. I was completely and utterly living in these stories and all the emotion that was embedded within them. Then, in line with the analysis approach I was adopting, I began to break the experiences apart to code the data. I started to unpack each and every point that the parents had shared and categorise them into groups and under headings. The stories became more distant, the emotion began to diminish, but my codes and eventually general dimensions began to develop. A succinct illustration of the core ideas shared by the parents was identified and key quotes that could provide emotive insight into the parents' experiences were selected. The two papers were published and, we hope, communicated valuable and important information regarding the experiences of tennis parents. Certainly, they helped to push forward our own thinking regarding parenting children in sport and remain a resource utilised by the Lawn Tennis Association, who funded the research.

On reflection, however, in producing these traditional scientific-style papers, a lot of the raw emotion that was evident in parents' writing and conversations was removed. Instead, the parents' experiences were considered as data that could be neatly categorised and presented. Much of what drew us into the data was diminished and, the question has to be asked, did we appropriately or fully represent what the parents had shared? Did we really give them a voice as we had hoped? Developing this creative nonfiction (CNF) story has enabled us to revisit the data and the papers, to consider them as a whole and to re-present the experiences that were shared with us. To maximise the opportunities to incorporate the emotion and reflection we felt in the original data, we have chosen to present a monologue from the perspective of one mother. Her conversations and thoughts are provided throughout, with her very personal, internal dialogue reflected through the use of italics.

Before progressing to the story, it is important to recognise that this CNF provides another interpretation of the original information and that it was impossible for us to consider our original two papers in isolation, given that we have both continued to conduct research in this area for a further 15 years. Thus, this re-presentation, while drawing heavily upon these initial two studies, is also informed by our ever-growing understanding of this extremely complex topic. Moreover, it is influenced by our own reflections and experiences as tennis players, which we both were when the studies were first conducted, and also parents, something which is more recent for both of us.

My Life in a Day as a Tennis Parent

The Organisational Challenge

Beep, Beep, Beep...BEEP, BEEP, BEEP...BEEEEEP, BEEEEEP, BEEEEEP...*alright, alright, alright, I'm up, I'm UP! How dare I ever contemplate a lazy Saturday morning!*

Reaching out to try and turn off the alarm, I smack my arm on the bedside unit and instantly feel it throbbing as another bruise adds to those from the previous mornings, *another great start to the day!* I can find the phone but where's the button to turn off this incessant noise that rudely awoke me from my slumber and only break I have from thinking about tennis?
Why can't I EVER find the button on this stupid stupid phone!

This stupid phone that I couldn't function without, that drives my life – quite literally! Directing me thousands of miles around the country, keeping track of our hugely complicated schedule, totalling up our never-ending expenses, those eye-watering expenses, *oh what I could do with that money if it wasn't all spent on tennis....*

Oh! don't start thinking about that so early in the morning, it's not even light out yet, and oh, GREAT! It's raining again, that's going to make for a fun drive. At least the tournament's indoors today, that's something I suppose....

Ah peace, finally, it's off!
I DREAD to think how bad the bags are today, maybe I'll just avoid all mirrors, if I don't know how tired I look maybe I won't feel it...?!

It's been a helluva week between county training, regional training, and individual lessons, the added bonus of multiple physio trips, late nights with school projects, and not to mention her brother's football match and school play. But it will be worth it; they say she needs it, they tell me she needs it; she needs the time on court, she needs the tournaments, she's not match fit because of the time off with her injury. Her coaches told me we need to get her playing some matches. I need to give her the opportunities, I don't want to be the reason she doesn't succeed, my tiredness isn't important, she HAS to come first, her tennis HAS to come first, she needs your support... *And right now, she needs you to GET OUT OF BED!!*

Ok, I'm back on my wheel, the world is turning again, we're back at it! Breakfast is done, well it is if you can call half a slice of barely touched toast and some orange juice breakfast. We sat in silence as Miri picked at her toast, as we always do on match days. I do NOT want to be responsible for saying the wrong thing and being blamed for a loss. Even Theo stays out the way; he knows not to mess up on match days. He's learnt his place, in the background, not causing a fuss, not asking for too much and just watching as his sister consumes more and more of my time and energy as she, *we(?), I(?), who knows at this stage,* try to help Miri, achieve her, *it is her's right?* dream, that ever so lofty dream of playing at Wimbledon.

Bags are packed and the car, our ever faithful, petrol guzzling estate, the favoured car of tennis parents around the country, is loaded. I fight the urge to ask Miri if she's remembered everything. She's 13 now and I just have to trust her. I can't keep reminding her to check her racquets and shoes, if she's forgotten something she'll just have to live with the consequences. She really does need to start taking some responsibility for herself, *I won't let myself be one of those parents trudging along behind her carrying her water bottle as she approaches adulthood.*

Miri's taken up her usual position, slumped in the back seat, headphones in, some crap game no doubt being playing on her phone. Her opponent's probably reading through her game plan and setting goals, having consumed a nutritious and energy filled bowl of porridge with dried fruit. But I won't mention that. I won't remind her what her coach said she should do on the way to matches, or what the sport psych suggested to help with her anxiety. I won't try and encourage her or make her feel more positive about the upcoming match. I learnt long ago that Miri does what Miri wants on match days. I'll do anything to keep the peace and minimise the inevitable post-match fall-out if she loses.

I turn on the engine and the car jumps into action, warm air blowing, windscreen wipers going, and some gentle classical music playing from the radio to help calm my nerves. It is nerves that I'm feeling, right...right?

What is the feeling? That nagging feeling like I've forgotten something. I've fed the cat, the oven is off, the door is locked, Dan is away at his corporate retreat (lucky him!), my laptop is packed, with my backlog of emails downloaded waiting for a response... what have I forgotten? Ah, it can't be that important, I'll just sort it when we get back, we're only away for a night thank goodness!

Oh Shit! Theo! I forgot Theo.

That poor kid, not again, how have I done it again?! HOW HAVE I DONE IT AGAIN?! Useless, just useless. Quick quick, turn around, maybe he won't have noticed we left...

Who am I kidding? Of course, he noticed we left; I left, with Miri, for the weekend, and I forgot him. He's at the door waiting. Yes, we were only down the road but that doesn't matter, I forgot him, and he knows it. The disappointment on his face as he once again realises that he's an afterthought to Miri's tennis breaks my heart. I'll have to make it up to him next week, Dan will HAVE to take Miri to one of her lessons, no matter how busy he is with work. I've got to fix this. *This can be fixed right? He's not going to hate me forever?*

Now we're running late, we need to get going!
"Hurry Theo!"
"Get in the car!"
"What were you doing? Why didn't you come out when we were leaving?!"
Oh great, good parenting! Now you're snapping at him when it's your fault we're running late. You forgot him! You were so focused on Miri that you forgot your own son! Don't make this even worse by blaming him. You're useless, not him.

Theo's been unceremoniously dumped with his friend and the usual pleasantries have been exchanged:
"Yes, we're off to a tournament with Miri *again*"

"Yes, it's only a few hours away, which is a nice change"

"No, we won't be going on holiday this year as Miri has nationals"

"Yes, we're very excited to see what Miri might achieve"

"Yes, we're very grateful that you are looking after Theo *again* and of course we'd love to reciprocate and have Ethan over one evening soon (*blatant lie*)."

"No, we won't be too late back tomorrow (*another blatant lie*)."

"Thank-you again"

"Oh, and Theo, here's some money for food and activities, be polite, don't get into trouble, and see you tomorrow."

We need to find some other friends to use for childcare, we're starting to push our luck with Ethan's family. Who haven't we used recently? If only my family were closer or more available. I can't wait until Theo is old enough to be left on his own… it will make all of this so much easier when I can just leave him at home alone…

Back on the road; fortunately, traffic is light and we sail through the usual hotspots for accidents and traffic jams. Despite my concerns about being late, we arrive at the venue, as usual, with plenty of time to spare. It's a nice club today, thankfully……*Not a freezing air bubble over Tarmac courts in sight, what a relief!* I'm always grateful when we're at a nice club, like this one, with plenty of space and chairs that are comfortable enough to sit on for 12 hours or so, big screen TVs showing various football matches that might distract some of the more sport-focused parents, and a kitchen serving food that is almost passable as healthy. *Good job since you didn't have time to make any lunch today!* A nice club can make even the worse of match days that little bit more bearable.

Dealing with Competition

Miri has gone off to sign in with the tournament referee and I've plonked myself and my laptop down at the nearest table, ready to try and get on with some work. Miri, as you might have guessed, likes to be left alone at this point and I like to avoid certain, *let's be honest, most*, other parents! Work is a perfect excuse. I put my headphones in, put my head down, and try to concentrate on the work I was meant to have completed days ago for my boss. But I'm distracted, I keep looking around waiting for Miri to return. Who is she playing I wonder? *It doesn't matter who she's playing, it's about getting back on court and gaining some match practice after the injury, remember, it doesn't matter who she's playing.*

Uh oh, look at that face. She's clearly got a bad draw. Deep breath, stay positive, don't get drawn into discussions about the opponent, help her stay focused on herself. Stay calm, stay calm, just stay calm!

"Ok Miri?"

"I've got her again, mum! I can't believe it, how have I got her again?
It's not fair mum, we've come all this way and I'm playing her again. It's a
fix, I swear it's a fix, just because she's their favourite, it's not fair. I don't
want to play her again."

*Oh Crap, Oh Crappy Crappy Crap. This is not going to be fun, not the
Jones.' I cannot deal with this kid, or her parents....Dammit, why did they
enter this tournament? I thought they'd be going to the Grade 2. Why are
they in a Grade 3? This was meant to be a nice ease back in for Miri, now
we've got to deal with them! Stay Calm, take a deep breath and just STAY
CALM!*

"You're playing Iris I take it?"

"Uh huh"

"Ok, well, you did well against her last time, you know what you need
to do to play well, and remember, you're just coming back from your injury so there's no pressure."

"Pressure! Of course there's pressure! (*Oh no, I said the wrong thing!
Why did I say so much?!*) Everyone will be looking, everyone will be
watching, everyone expects me to win, but she cheats and she hacks and I
hate it. And everyone will be watching. The coaches will know, they will
know when I lose, they know I can't beat her. I'll just get angry when she
cheats. She cheats mum! She always cheats! And she doesn't play good
tennis, she just lobs the ball up in the air! How am I meant to play well
against that? How can I play good tennis against her? We might as well go
home now. What's the point? They all love her but she's rubbish. She just
wins by playing rubbish tennis and they all think it's amazing!"

*What to say, what to say, what to say? She's spiralling, her anxiety is
going to get the better of her. What do I focus on? Do I tell her she doesn't
cheat, when she clearly does (and her parents know and even encourage
it)? Do I tell her it doesn't matter, when it clearly matters to her? Do I tell
her just to enjoy it, when nothing about this match is going to be enjoyable
for either of us? What do I say? Help me, someone help me!!! WHAT DO
I SAY????*

"I'm sorry Miri, I was hoping Iris would be at the Grade 2"

"Well she's not is she, she's here and I'm playing her"

And it's clearly my fault...Strike one

"It's a tough draw Miri, I'm sorry. But remember, you haven't played a
match for a good few months, so no one is expecting anything."

"Oh, so you think I'm going to lose?"

...Strike 2

"No, of course not. That's not what I said. I just think it's important to remember that you haven't been able to play a lot recently and that we've just come here to try and get some match practice. Try and focus on your own game and the things you've been working on this week with Tim."

"Tim's useless, all he wants me to do is practice my serve but my serve is fine, it's my backhand I need to work on, I can't hit any backhands in, I might as well just aim for the back fence every time..."

Strike 3 and I give up. I can't win here. Nothing's going to be right, she's already lost before she's gone on. Another wasted Saturday. Oh, I'm so glad we came! It's not like I might want to do anything else with my day like, sleep, tidy up, relax, catch up with work, see some friends, spend time with Dan, remind Theo that he is valued and loved as a child....

I better shift to neutral ground.

"Ok Miri, would you like a drink before you go on?"
I'd like a drink, a very very big drink...but it's only 8 am, the bar's not open yet and even if it were I'm not sure the other parents would think much of me drinking at 8 am. Well actually they might if they knew which parents I now had to go and watch with....but coffee it will have to be. There better be coffee...

MIRABEL RICHARDS AND IRIS JONES, MIRABEL RICH-ARDS AND IRIS JONES, PLEASE REPORT TO THE REFEREE'S DESK READY FOR PLAY
Oh, here we go, not even time to get a coffee and she's called to play. At least that means we're starting on time, that's something I guess!
"Good luck Miri, have fun"
"WHAT?"
Oh not fun, she hates it when you say have fun.
"Good luck Miri, play well"
Good correction, smooth, that's better.
"I'll play as well as I can against this hacker, make sure you watch out for her cheating"

Oh good, she's in a perfect frame of mind for this match! At least she's gone on now, nothing I can do about what's about to happen. I wish I didn't have to watch, but she'll be looking for me. Time to get my game face on. Just please Iris, please please please, I'm begging you, don't cheat, play decent tennis, don't mess Miri about. I CANNOT deal with another disappointment, I NEVER say the right thing and the anger, oh the anger is just too much to manage.

I take a deep breath, plaster a smile onto my face, and look around, frantically trying to locate one of the parents I like. I need someone to talk to, someone to help me calm down and to distract me while Miri and Iris warm-up. I spot Mr Lewis, newspaper in one hand, coffee in the other, looking, as always, like he hasn't got a care in the world. *Oh, if only!* I give him an enthusiastic wave and rapidly start to walk towards him, hoping to avoid anything more than a polite acknowledgement of other parents I pass on the way.

I like Mr Lewis. He's like me; he keeps himself to himself and tries to steer clear of the politics. We often laugh about being the outcasts of the tennis world; our daughters aren't good enough for us to be invited into the "funded players" clique, but they take it too seriously for us to be part of the "tennis is just a fun past time and way to have holidays" group. We live in a strange sort of purgatory; we've committed too much and for too long to just give it all up, to pull the support that would signal the end of our daughters' dreams. We're not brave enough, or perhaps honest enough, to tell them they haven't quite got what it takes to reach the heady heights of professional tennis, *or maybe we're just hanging onto the hope that maybe, just maybe, they are…*. But we are such a long way from this just being fun. It's all consuming; mentally, physically, financially. We live, breath, and eat tennis and yes, we can see our daughters' gaining a whole lot of benefits from playing, but is it worth the stress it causes us? *No, it's absolutely not…who am I even trying to kid that the benefits might outweigh this continual mental torture?*

"Mr Lewis, Rhys! Hello! How are you?"

"Jaime, how lovely to see you. I am well, thank-you. How are you? How's Miri's shoulder?"

"We are fine thanks. Miri's shoulder seems to be, fingers crossed, doing ok. She's been back training for a couple of weeks, so we'll see how it holds up today. How's Jane? Is she playing already?"

"Jane's doing really well thanks, she's had a couple of good runs recently, finally beat Amy, did you hear? Bit of a shock for all of us, but great for her to finally have that monkey off her back!"

"Oh! That's great news, I'm so pleased for her, I bet she was delighted. Fingers crossed for something similar for us today, Miri's just gone on against Iris"

"Oh…"

"Yep…"

"Are her…"

"Yes, planted themselves behind the court already, of course, got to have the best view in the house!"

"Of course, of course!"

"Could have done without it today if I'm honest"

"Oh, I bet! Could do without that draw any day. You want to stay down here with me, out the way?"

"I wish I could, but Miri will be expecting to see me. In fact, I better head back towards the court, don't want her panicking before the match has even started."

"Ok, well, let me go and get you a coffee at least!"

"Oh, that would be amazing, thank-you so much. A small black Americano would be fabulous…a shot of whiskey too if you can find one, you know, to calm the nerves!"

"Hahahah, I'll see what I can do!"

I glance across at Miri's court, I see them at the net, spinning the racquet to decide who'll serve first. *Come on Miri, have a good game, come on. I know you can do it, I know you can, just stay calm, play your game, don't get sucked into the cheating and the hacking, stick to what you know. And whatever you do, do not look at her parents….*

0–3 already. It's only been 8 minutes and Miri's already lost her serve twice, thrown her racquet, smacked her leg, and threatened to call the referee over a bad line call. So, it's going about as well as I expected! I know the other parents are looking, I can feel their eyes burning into my head; judging Miri's poor behaviour, questioning my parenting. *If only they knew! This is good compared to what she used to be like! I've tried everything; stopping competitions, focusing on enjoyment, working with a sport psych. She's just passionate and wants it all to be perfect. She hasn't worked out how to control all the emotions that rage through her yet. She'll get there in the end, I know she will… well, she better get there in the end!*

2–3, she's broken back. *Thank goodness for that, she's on the scoreboard!* She's calming down and starting to find her groove. She even seems to have remembered her between points routine. *Breathe, I can breathe, at least for a minute.*

2–5. Well, that didn't last long! Two bad line calls, a lucky winner and any semblance of control is gone. I won't be surprised if she gets a code violation soon, if she carries on like this. *It's really not her fault though, Iris' line calls are terrible, and she was doing so well before that, trying so hard to keep calm and keep fighting. Should I do something? Find the referee? I know I'm not meant to get involved, it's meant to be down to Miri to sort but she's only 13 and this is already ridiculous…I can't just stand by and watch this match get ripped away from Miri because of cheating… Where is that useless referee anyway? Surely he should be here, next to the court, they all know Iris cheats. If he just stood here, by the court, Iris might not do it and then maybe, just maybe, we could all have an enjoyable match.*

2–6, first set is over. It was a disastrous last game; one return hitting the back netting, another straight into the bottom of the net, a shanked backhand wide, and an easy forehand long. Iris is elated, beaming as she heads towards the net to get ready for the next set. As usual, her parents are celebrating like she just won Wimbledon, clapping and cheering, any attempts to respect tennis etiquette well and truly out the window.

Oh, my poor Miri, it hasn't even been a close set, it really doesn't warrant all this commotion! It's ok, Miri. It doesn't matter, it's ok. You can still do this, you can, I believe in you, I'll always believe in you. Just find a way, you can find a way…I know you can.

I can feel Miri searching for me, searching for some reassurance. I wish there was something I could do, anything at all… It's just like watching her sit a maths exam and put all the wrong answers in! I wish I could swoop on court and give her a big hug, tell her it's all ok, that she doesn't have to keep playing, that I love her no matter what happens, that tennis isn't all that important. I wish I could send someone else on to replace her or give her the answers. *I wish, I wasn't here. I wish I wasn't watching. I wish…I just wish she wasn't playing Iris.* But, there's nothing I can do. My little girl is out there, all on her own, with nowhere to hide; every mistake exposed, every emotion visible for all to see. All I can do is stand here, a smile on my face, clapping her good shots, and sending her positive vibes. All I can do is hope. Hope she can find her game, hope she can stay calm, hope she manages to smile at least once during this match.

The second set has started better. A great first game for Miri, two aces and a backhand winner. She's not giving up! She's come out ready to fight! I am so proud of her! *Here we go Miri, here we go, you got this!!!*

Yes Miri, what a game! That'll show her, all that celebrating at the end of the set! What a game, what a game!! 2–0, you're on a roll, well done my darling girl!

3–0 and Miri's cruising! I don't know how she's done it, but she's completely turned it around. She's gained control, she's walking with purpose, with intent. She's striding around the court, questioning Iris' calls, taking control of the points. She's just amazing. I am so, so, so impressed by her. Go Miri.

4–1. Ok. She's got one back, but it's just one. Miri's still leading and, most importantly, she's still looking confident. She's still taking the ball on, seeking to dominate the games. Most importantly, she's still got her racquet in her hand rather than smashed across the floor.

Yes! 6–1. What a set! What a wonderful set to watch. Well Done, Miri!

Stay calm, stay in control. Smile but nothing more. Do not distract Miri, do not let on how you are feeling. Do not give Mr and Mrs Jones any sort of satisfaction, they mustn't know that you are excited Miri has won a set. And I mustn't take satisfaction in the fact the smile has been wiped off their faces... ok, take only a little satisfaction that the smile has been wiped off their faces.

Here we go then. One set all, the deciding set ahead. Deep breath, big smile. Focus!

1–0
1–1
2–1
2–2
3–2
3–3

Come on Miri, just keep holding your serve! Just breath, deep breath, just breath.

Double fault, love fifteen.

Deep breath, doesn't matter, it's just one point.

Fifteen all, lovely forehand down the line. Well Done, Miri!

Thirty, fifteen. Sneaky dropshot off the defensive.

Fourty, Fifteen...no, what. Thirty all, it's not thirty all. *Miri, don't fall for it, don't fall for it. Stand your ground, it's forty fifteen, you know it's forty fifteen. Come on Iris, not now, not now! Oh, this is unbelievable, it's clearly forty fifteen, Miri's won three points this game, it's game point. It's not thirty all. Come on ref, come on, intervene, please intervene...where are you Ref? What's the point of you if you don't intervene now?*

Thirty all (*WHAT?!*)
30–40.
Game.
3–4.

Oh Miri, I'm so sorry. I'm so sorry it's happened again. Please don't give up, please don't let her get to you. Don't let her win. You can still do this, I know you can still do this.

3–5.
3–6.
Game.
Set.
Match.
It's all over.

It's all over. Take a breath Miri, take a breath. Don't get upset, please don't get upset. Hold it together, just hold it together until we're in the car.

Don't let them see you upset, don't be upset. Miri it's just a game, oh my darling girl, it's just a game. Please, please, please, smile, shake hands, hold it together. Just hold it together.

Quick, to the car. Head down, jacket on, get to the car. We avoid all the looks, all the words of sympathy. We just focus on getting to the car. We can both breathe again once we get to the car.

I yank open the door, the door to our faithful car, that's seen us through every win and every loss, every disappointment and success. Our faithful car, Miri's sanctuary, her peace, her place.

Miri's shoulder sink, her head drops, her hands raise and the shaking starts. The heart wrenching shoulder shakes are accompanied by silent sobs. I sit in silence, just as I started the day. I don't know what to say.

Why don't I ever know what to say? What can you say? I've just seen my daughter get destroyed in front of me. She tried so hard, she did so well. She came back and she fought. She lost but I don't care that she lost. I wouldn't care if she never won another tennis match again. She's just so sad. My darling girl is devastated, and I can't fix it. I don't have the words to make her feel better right now. I know it's just one tennis match, I know it's just a game, but it's so much more than that for her. It's her everything. Right now, in this moment, it's her everything, and her everything just fell apart and I just stood on the balcony and watched.

Fears for the Future

So that's it, then, another ride on the emotional rollercoaster complete, and another one to look forward to later today – the consolation draw (although it's no consolation to Miri)! There were some highs; the joy of watching Miri fight and chase down every ball, seeing her break out into a smile as she hit that backhand winner to close out the second set, and the relief that her injury held up. But these highs pale in comparison to the lows; seeing Miri once again destroyed at the end of a match, seeing her unsuccessfully fight against bad line calls and changes to the score, watching her try with every ounce of her being to hold it together before, once more, sitting in silence as tears streamed down her face while all I could do was wait for the pain and disappointment to subside.

Her pain or my pain? I hurt so much for her. Am I failing her? I'm her mum, I should protect her from disappointment and upset, take away tears and sadness but instead I merrily sign her up for it. I facilitate this pain, I pay for it, I take her to it, I put other things, important things, on hold so that she can experience it. I do everything to help her with her tennis but am I really just setting her up for heartbreak? Heartbreak that I then can't fix. I don't have the words to make her feel better. I don't have the means to comfort her or help her see perspective. I simply exist, helpless, hopeless, useless.

"Why do we do it?" I ask Dan when I call him to give him the update. "Why do we put ourselves through it?" "Why do we put Miri through it?" "Why don't we just stop?" We could have holidays, and family time. Miri could see her friends. Theo could have some attention. I could finally catch up on work. Dan and I could, do I dare even think it, spend some time together. We could relax. We could breathe. We could smile.

So why don't we just stop? How could I? We're trapped, by the game, by the system, by Miri's desire. This has been our life for the last seven years. Training and tournaments; ratings and rankings. We've searched for the best coaches, equipment, and competitions. We've read books and magazines and watched videos. We've observed others and talked to parents (those we like anyway!). We've made mistake after mistake after mistake, but we're learning. We're getting better. We're figuring it out. We're trying. We're doing the best we can. And that's all we can do for Miri. That's all I can expect from her....and it's all I can expect from us...right...

But have we done enough? Are we doing enough? Is it enough? Have we learnt enough? Have we made the right decisions? Did we go wrong long ago or are we on the right path? Is there a right path? Is there even a path? Are the decisions we make now helping Miri for the long-term or screwing her up completely? Oh, how would I know?!

Ok, it's time to stop that now. This isn't the time for reflection, for worrying about what's been and what's to come. Now it's time to pull it together. It's time to move on. Miri has to move on, you have to move on. There's another match ahead.

There's always another match. Another tournament. Another day.

Reflective Questions

1   How does this creative nonfiction fit with your or your parents' experiences of youth sport?
2   Based on this story, how would you now describe the experience of youth sport parents?
3   Could the experience parents have within youth sports, such as tennis, influence how they engage with their children? How?
4   What changes within youth sport might help to make the experience of parents more positive or enjoyable?

References

Baxter-Jones, A.D., Maffulli, N., & TOYA Study Group. (2003). Parental influence on sport participation in elite young athletes. *The Journal of Sports Medicine and Physical Fitness, 43*, 250–255.

Burgess, N. S., Knight, C. J., & Mellalieu, S. D. (2016). Parental stress and coping in elite youth gymnastics: An interpretative phenomenological analysis. *Qualitative Research in Sport, Exercise, and Health, 8*, 237–256. http://dx.doi.org/10.1080/2159676X.2015.1134633

Côté, J. (1999). The influence of the family in the development of talent in sport. *The Sport Psychologist, 13*, 395–417. https://doi.org/10.1123/tsp.13.4.395

Fredricks, J. A., & Eccles, J. S. (2004). Parental influences on youth involvement in sports. In M. R. Weiss (Ed.), *Developmental sport and exercise psychology: A lifespan perspective* (pp. 144–164). Morgantown, WV: Fitness Information Technology.

Harwood, C. G., Drew, A., & Knight, C. J. (2010). Parental stressors in professional youth football academies: A qualitative investigation in specializing stage parents. *Qualitative Research in Sport and Exercise Sciences, 2*, 39–55. http://dx.doi.org/10.1080/19398440903510152

Harwood, C., & Knight, C. J. (2009a). Understanding parental stressors: An investigation of British tennis-parents. *Journal of Sports Sciences, 27*, 339–351. http://dx.doi.org/10.1080/02640410802603871

Harwood, C., & Knight, C. J. (2009b). Stress in youth sport: A developmental investigation of tennis parents. *Psychology of Sport and Exercise, 10*, 447–456. http://dx.doi.org/10.1016/j.psychsport.2009.01.005

Harwood, C. G., & Knight, C. J. (2015). Parenting in youth sport: A position paper on parenting expertise. *Psychology of Sport & Exercise, 16*, 24–35. http://dx.doi.org/10.1016/j.psychsport.2014.03.001

Harwood, C. G., Thrower, S. N., Slater, M. J., Didymus, F. F., & Frearson, L. (2019). Advancing our understanding of psychological stress and coping among parents in organized youth sport. *Frontiers in Psychology, 10*. https://doi.org/10.3389/fpsyg.2019.01600

Hayward, F. P. I., Knight, C. J., & Mellalieu, S. D. (2017). A longitudinal examination of stressors, appraisal, and coping in youth swimming. *Psychology of Sport and Exercise, 29*, 56–68. http://dx.doi.org/10.1016/j.psychsport.2016.12.002

Kirk, D., Carlson, T., O'Connor, A., Burke, P., Davis, K., & Glover, S. (1997a). The economic impact on families of children's participation in junior sport. *Australian Journal of Science and Medicine in Sport, 29*, 27–33.

Kirk, D., O'Connor, A., Carlson, T., Burke, P., Davis, K., & Glover, S. (1997b). Time commitments in junior sport: Social consequences for participants and their families. *European Journal of Physical Education, 2*(1), 51–73. https://doi.org/10.1080/1740898970020105

Knight, C. J., Berrow, S. R., & Harwood, C. G. (2017). Parenting in sport. *Current Opinion in Psychology, 16*, 93–97. https://doi.org/10.1016/j.copsyc.2017.03.011

Leinhart, N., Nicaise, V., Knight, C. J., & Guillet-Descas, E. (2020). Understanding parental stressors and coping experiences in elite sport contexts. *Sport, Exercise, and Performance Psychology, 9*(3), 390–404. https://doi.org/10.1037/spy0000186

Wolfenden, L. E., & Holt, N. L. (2005). Talent development in elite junior tennis: Perceptions of players, parents and coaches. *Journal of Applied Sport Psychology, 17*, 108–126. http://dx.doi.org/10.1080/10413200590932416

Wylleman, P., & Rosier, N. (2016). Holistic perspective on the development of elite athletes. In M. Raab, P. Wylleman, R. Seiler, A.-M. Elbe, & A. Hatzigeorgiadis (Eds.), *Sport and exercise psychology research* (pp. 269–288). Academic Press.

4 (Re)Assembling 'Balance'

A Creative Nonfiction of Athlete Mothers Negotiating Sport and Family

Kerry R. McGannon and Jenny McMahon

Introduction

In the present creative nonfiction, we draw on findings from a published study titled 'Juggling Motherhood and Sport: A Qualitative Study of the Negotiation of Competitive Athlete Mother Identities' (McGannon, McMahon, & Gonsalves, 2018). In this work, we explored competitive recreational athlete mother (i.e., women who compete in races outside of elite sport training and competition) identities in relation to strategies used to negotiate training and family spheres. Focusing on physically active mothers is important to learn more about how they navigate psychological, social, and cultural barriers that constrain physical activity (McGannon, McMahon, & Gonsalves, 2017). Once becoming mothers, women are subjected to cultural ideals that stress that in order to attain a 'good mother identity' they should place family needs above their own, including physical activity pursuits (Miller & Brown, 2005). These 'good mother' ideals are the product of individual, social, and cultural discourses, which create particular identity meanings and associated practices (Vair, 2013). To align with this conception of motherhood, we used 'discursive psychology' (McGannon & Mauws, 2000) to explore competitive athlete mother identities as interdependent with language and social action (McGannon et al., 2017; McGannon & Smith, 2015). Using this theoretical focus expands understanding of athlete mothers' physical activity participation, within the context of work-leisure balance, and cultural discourses.

Within our study, seven North American women 39–42 years of age (mean age 40.5 years), from multiple sports (e.g., triathlon, running, mountain biking) shared their journeys as athlete mothers (McGannon et al., 2018). All participants were able-bodied with male partners, two children with at least one child under the age of six, worked 20–45 hours per week, and devoted 8–15 hours or more per week to training depending on time of year (i.e., training increased at certain points in some training cycles). Athlete mothers' journeys were obtained using open-ended interview questions developed from the literature and contextual knowledge of the first author, but also allowed participants to direct conversations in

DOI: 10.4324/9781003038900-7

personally meaningful ways (Smith & Sparkes, 2016). Participants were invited to talk about their lives as athletes and mothers (e.g., tell me about your journey as an athlete and a mother, tell me about your motivations and inspirations) and reflect on the positives and challenges. Interviews lasted between 90 and 210 minutes per session.

The interviews were subjected to a reflexive form of thematic analysis (Braun, Clarke, & Weate, 2016) to identify discourses and strategies participants used to negotiate identities as mothers and athletes. The findings gleaned from our analysis built on qualitative research on physically active mothers that has shown recreational sport allows for personal, social, and cultural barriers to be renegotiated in ways that facilitate well-being and sport participation (Batey & Owton, 2014; McGannon et al., 2017; Spowart, Burrows, & Shaw, 2010). A key finding was that women strove to balance identities – competitive athlete and good mother – to uphold harmony within the family (Vair, 2013), within a central theme called 'juggling motherhood and sport'. This central theme allowed us to show how training and competitive goals uphold, and transform, parental responsibilities in ways that were compatible with sport. This central theme also showed the nuanced ways in which athlete mothers 'juggled' – and struggled with – discourses of good motherhood and/or a discourse of balance that suggests they do it all on their own with ease (McGannon & Schinke, 2013).

In what follows, we shift from 'story analysts' to 'storytellers' (Smith, 2016). The position of a storyteller was made possible by selecting compelling passages from the data to communicate findings within the context of the central theme of 'juggling motherhood and sport'. In so doing, we created stories that show the nuanced ways in which 'juggling motherhood and sport' is constraining and emancipative, related to three strategies women used to negotiate identities as athlete mothers. These strategies included: (1) adjustment of training and competition; (2) support as multifaceted and negotiated; and (3) reciprocity of motherhood and sport (McGannon et al., 2018). This 'creative nonfiction' (CNF) process involved centralizing meaningful experiences of participants, through creating fictional storylines using creative writing practices related to the research questions from our realist tale (McMahon, 2016; Smith, McGannon, & Williams, 2016). As storytellers, we sought to transform our realist tale findings, by bringing competitive athlete mothers' subjectivities 'to life' through a theoretical lens (Frank, 2010), in a way that may resonate with readers through witnessing the stories (Carless & Douglas, 2016).

To accomplish this goal, the overarching theme and strategies identified in the realist tale are presented in the form of CNF vignettes. Vignettes are brief evocative and compelling storied descriptions of research findings (Spalding & Phillips, 2007). Within CNF research, three types of vignettes have been used: (a) portrait (i.e., narrative sketches provide insight into individual participant's character and lives), (b) snapshot (i.e., narrative sketches capture observed experiences within a particular time and setting), and (c) composite (i.e., creation of one narrator or set of experiences to centralize a story) (Spalding & Phillips, 2007). We constructed composite vignettes to synthesize women's voices into shared powerful accounts, using one character telling a fluid story across time and space. The intent with these vignettes is to show the strategies within the central theme of juggling motherhood and sport as laden with nuanced tensions. Although we used creative license as storytellers, rigour was enhanced by integrating quotes, direct phrases, and exact wording from the interview data, to centralize participants' voices and experiences (Smith et al., 2016). In the following six composite vignettes, the women's ways of speaking are thus kept 'in-tact', to retain authenticity of their experiences (Carless & Douglas, 2016; Smith et al., 2016).

Juggling Motherhood and Sport: Six Composite Vignettes of Balance

Vignette 1: Balance Is a Juggling Act, with Rubber and Glass Balls

Sport really is important, it's a big part of my life, even more so, since becoming a parent. If it wasn't in my life, it would be 100% about being a mum, along with work and career. I'm not saying that kids and family aren't important, but I'm not going to be of use to anyone, if I can't do what I love – and that's train and compete in my sport. If you wanna do all of that stuff, it's a balancing game. Sometimes it isn't even that you want to do all that stuff, but it's expected you do all that stuff, or you give something up if you can't balance it. I love my family and work so it's not like I am going to give that up, so when you become a mum, you sometimes think "maybe I won't want to keep training anymore, maybe I won't need to" and "maybe being a parent will be the next phase, and sport will be behind me". Then you find you come back to sport, a little bit here and a bit there, and soon you are training and competing again, and it's challenging and amazing! With being a mum, and all that rest of the stuff on the plate that goes along with it, something has got to give. I guess it feels like juggling, trying to fit all in. But it's also "an act", in the sense you are keeping all these balls in the air and people think "you're a pretty good juggler of all those balls – good job, keeping going". Juggling all those balls is an illusion – because it's hard work and practice, to keep them in the air – people don't see the work. It's also really hard sometimes to keep them all in the air if more and more balls keep getting added, into the juggling act.

What I've learned – and it's been through trial and error – with trying to balance work, relationship, kids, training, and racing – is that I'm juggling different types of balls – rubber balls and glass balls. Some things are more like 'rubber balls' which if those balls fall, they won't break, they bounce back. Like for me, cooking, cleaning, and day to day home stuff – sometimes it can be pushed aside. Even if I leave those things for a bit, they bounce back eventually. The laundry will pile up sure, but it will get done, and life goes on. Even with cooking there are ways around that, like it does not always have to be perfect, my partner and kids are pretty easy on that. Some work stuff is like that too, where if you leave it or even drop it, it will bounce back. That's not always the case with work, and that's where it gets hard, because you realize that some balls are more fragile, like glass. Glass balls can get cracks, and if they do, they won't be strong enough, and eventually some might even break, especially when you're juggling. It might be different for every mum, but for me, my relationship and kids could be like glass balls, if I get stretched too thin and even if the balance was good at one point, it becomes like a juggling act, if I'm trying to do all this when it isn't possible. I can't keep those glass balls in the air, and if they drop, they can't be repaired and it's a whole chain reaction for them, and for me too.

Sport and training for me, can sometimes be a glass ball, even though I might think or want it to be, a rubber ball. I remember the first race I did, when I was doing all the training when my daughter was younger and after my son was born. I was lifting her off somewhere while I did the really hard work of training, like running and swimming. And that sounds all grand and whatever, and people would say to me, "I don't know you how you do it – you are a super mum"! Well, I mean, this is what I do, it's what we do as a family. There is sport for mum. The reality was that to make that happen, I have to get up at 4 am to do the run before the family wakes up, or go to the pool at a time that I don't like, because work was scheduled so that is the 'best time' to go. So, yea...then tending to the business, and also trying to find relationship time, because that is important. At a certain point... I felt like I was not where I wanna be, with being a good mum, partner, or with sport training, and I would feel guilty and defeated. Some days I'd ponder giving something up, but felt pulled in many directions, unsure of which direction was the clear path of balance. What should I give up? I would think, "hey, maybe if I put the training aside and just focus on my daughter then maybe I will feel better". I tried to do that. At first the down time was good, but pretty soon I'd feel restless and more stressed. I would think "I don't wanna be here doing only that either, I really miss running and competing". So you are damned if you do, damned if you don't. I felt guilty having to choose between the two... like I just... was miserable.

I love my family and I enjoy training and if I *had* to choose a rubber ball that could be dropped, it would be training and competing. I *could* let that go for a while and *maybe* it would bounce back. Maybe. But like I said, I miss it after a while, and I don't feel like quite myself. But family and the kids – I would not want to risk having cracks in, or even break, one of those glass balls. The whole 'either or' is bullshit and doesn't work. Eventually what I realized is that I *want* to do both – it's not as simple as just putting one aside and now you are a perfect parent. People say that you can do sport sure, but they will still make comments if they think you are training over spending time with the family. The sport and training look like 'self-time' and I guess it is, but it's not selfish, and my family doesn't see it that way. My sport is sometimes a glass ball that can also be a rubber ball, that is juggled, but in a good way. I have found ways to change my perspective and look closely at what I wanted – being a good mum and partner, involved with career, and training for races. In pursuing something, you're always going to have to say no to other things, and so you might not keep a perfectly clean house, or be as social, or you might not cook from scratch every night. You kind of find a balance by letting go of some things that might not be ideal, in order to pursue your overall goals. As soon as I hit the start line of a race, I'm just as motivated as ever to do as well as I can. That's because I'm competitive, it hasn't gone away just because I'm a mum, and so the juggling is worth it. I get to pursue my sport goals.

Adjustment of Training and Competition

Vignette 2: Wake Up, Plan, Train, Repeat – But Be Flexible

When I first came back to running after giving birth, I was running two days a week, and within six months I was up to four days a week and eventually got myself back up to six and seven days. It took time and effort, but eventually I did it and it does fluctuate depending on the season and training goals, but I am pretty consistent. How do I do it, how do I keep consistent? Well it's a bit like that movie 'Ground Hog Day' where the guy wakes up every day and finds that his life is on a repeat of the same day, with the chance to do it over. There are some slight changes but most of the day is pretty much the same. That is how some days have to be figured out when juggling motherhood and sport if you are going to: (1) stay sane and not feel guilty, (2) keep the family happy, and (3) get the training in that you need for improvement and competing. After I was up to a good base of three or four days a week, it took time to figure out when the best time is to run, how long I can run, based on the kids and their schedules. I had to plan, but also be flexible with the timing and quality of my runs. It might not sound like a big deal, but those things were different than before I became a parent and also different from when we had just one child. Before I became a mum there were more windows of time and more time that could be taken for granted during and after a workout session. With the first child, we had more time because it was just one kid to take care of instead of two, and both of us are active and wanted to fit training in. Things could be switched off between the two of us as parents.

But with the second child, we needed to be more strategic in order to get the training in. What does that look like? Six o'clock in the morning I am up and getting ready to go because everyone is still sleeping. My kids thankfully are not morning kids, but if they were, I could always go earlier. They don't usually get up at 6 o'clock so I leave around 6:30 am, and back at 8:30. By 8:30 am they're up and sort of banging around downstairs. They can watch T.V., or they can play a quiet game, they are pretty good that way. They are just waking up at that point anyway. I get in from my workout, have a quick shower, my husband can go get his run or whatever, and then I am on duty. And the day goes on from there. There's something to be said about getting your workout in first thing in the morning 'cause it's off your plate when you do it first thing, and you're more time efficient. Also taking your shower afterwards as quick as you can because you've got to get the kids off to school, plus get ready for work, so now it's done.

Sometimes a double workout is scheduled – like two in one day – things go similarly, around planning and getting it done efficiently, but with flexibility. On those days I get up, around 4:30 am and go to the pool to get a swim in before work. I get back in time to shower, eat and the kids are still not up, so I sometimes get a bit of 'me' time for a coffee. Then in the afternoons, depending on if my son was napping when I got home from work, I would try to get a second workout in. Otherwise I would do it after he went to bed at night. And then on the weekends, it was the same thing. I got up really early and got a workout in and then if he was napping, I'd try to workout at nap time or after he went to bed. Clearly – thank god for napping – as it worked well when they were younger. Now the kids are a bit older and don't take naps, so the workouts shift a bit, but you still need to plan, train, and figure that out, in relation to all the stuff you're trying to balance. So timing is still key, but my workouts are quality workouts, where everything has a purpose. There are no 'trash' or 'junk' workouts like you used to do before you had kids. You don't just do it to put the time in, everything I do is specific, with the idea it might have to change depending on the kids. I don't always prefer a certain time, but it's maybe the only time. So once again, get up in the morning and it's like "Okay, I know I have to go to track and get this done. This is how I'm going to fit it in. This is how I'm gonna do it". You know, "How do we run when the kids are around? Who's got the kids?" So that gets planned, changed if needed, and then away we go again!

Vignette 3: If They're Okay, I'm Okay

My personal philosophy is that I want to enjoy every minute of my life, but saying that and doing that with the demands of work, family, and number of hours in a day, do not make that straightforward. When it comes to training and competing, and being a parent, basically as long as they're happy, I'm happy. It they are doing okay, then I'm doing okay. If that ever changes, then I'd have to revaluate things. That sounds simpler compared to how it plays out in my mind and in real life. If I am going to continue with training and have performance goals and compete in races, then I make sure that the family's needs are taken care of. In order for my training to be worth it, I want to see improvements in my times and placements in races. If it's not fun, I don't want to do it, and part of that fun is when you see results, and it's really fun when you see your family cheering for you. None of that will be worth it if that happens at the expense of my kids or partner not having me around or missing quality family time. Mum guilt is real, but also, there are things that I do to try to alleviate stress on the family, including careful selection of the races I enter. My husband and I look at the season and figure out what races are nearby that won't take a lot of time away from everyone. These decisions are discussed as a team, but sometimes I still feel guilty for going. When the kids were younger the family would come to the race, usually at the end, and see mummy cross the finish line, that made it worth it. This made me happy, not just because I feel supported, but because I want them to view me as a role model. It can't be just about 'me' and training, even though I want to have it in my life. My family knows it is special, and we try to find ways that everyone can benefit, at least I hope so. I want them to get something out of it too, whether its family time or them being proud of mum.

I have also chosen races on the basis of the location and/or the timing, because I don't want to miss out on things that are important to my kids and the milestones in their lives. Recently I was like "I wanna pick a Spring marathon with a fast course". I found one that was flat and just so perfect, and then I was like "No damn, I can't, that's the same weekend as the swim meet for my daughter". Now that race is off the list, so you make a different choice – and it's a choice – not a sacrifice, because I can always find cool races to do on another day. I do not want to miss any of her events, or she would be upset, and I want to be there to see my daughter swim. I have recently done some crucial races away from home, and while those are rarer, thank god for technology like face time or other virtual ways to connect. This way they still see me and I still see them, even if I am only gone overnight or for a weekend race or whatever. Other times, we choose trips or family time where training or racing can be incorporated, with the kids coming along. We joke now that a lot of races I really want to do, are now slotted in as vacation time for the family, if they are in the summer.

As they are getting older, they are asking more questions about my races, and that makes me even more motivated to improve to make them proud. I know they are proud of me regardless, which is cool, but I want to continue to inspire my kids. I want them to see that mum doesn't have to give up everything, that she can do sport, and is strong. I have found that planning for what works best as a family, ended up taking away some of my guilt, whereas if I were to be doing a lot of my workouts with others when I could be at home with the kids, or doing a race instead of attending an event important to my child or the family, I'd feel guilty. Every year I re-evaluate where I am at in relation to the family. If I'm still enjoying it and my family's still okay with it, then I'll continue. This is my mindset: each year I revisit, "Am I still motivated, still enjoying it, and does it still work for the family?"

Support as Multifaceted and Negotiated

Vignette 4: We're in This Together, but Sometimes It's Hard to Say 'Yes'

It takes a whole village to raise a family, never mind a family that does sports, right? So, if there's a will to compete for athlete mums, there's a way to make it happen, hopefully with the help of that village. If I decide to do something in terms of training for a specific race or whatever, our entire family rallies around it. Without a partner who really 'gets' all this, I could not have started my training as a mum, let alone kept up with it, and reached the goals that I have. He understood my desire and goals to train and enter races, and he had an openness to prioritizing my training. And not just in words of support or like just saying 'good job' or 'good luck', but in real partnership and things that he did and still does, to make it happen and demonstrate he gets it and cares. He's probably one of my biggest cheerleaders and my biggest support in that sense. He would either fit his own workouts in around my training, or we would figure it out together, and do trade-offs. And that made some of my pressures and stress of being a mum and trying to juggle work and training, a bit easier, because there was rarely a conflict or resistance of "who's gonna go for a run" or "who's bike ride is most important". There was always some give and take to that and we'd figure it out in a supportive way "what's best for the kids", "when should I go out", "when should you go out". If there were times when the kids were more in need of me, like with feeding or fussiness, during those times, I would be there and then we would just trade off. He'd take the baby while I'm racing, and then also help with washing my bike. That's just another level of tiredness after you've done a race, that you don't have to deal with.

Of course, the other side to the 'village supports the athlete mum' idea, has been that sometimes I feel guilty to ask for help or take it when it was offered or available. I remember one time when my son was younger, I was tired and did not want to leave the house. We went to my parent's house for dinner and before leaving our dog took a shit on the carpet. I was like, "oh god, kill me now, I'm so done" and I wanted to cancel dinner, go to bed, and sleep. But I can't say "no" to my parents, so we went over there. My parents said at one point "Let us help". I'm like "No, I don't need help, I'm good, it's under control", even though it clearly was not. My mum's so supportive, even though she thinks I'm insane, she's very involved with the kids' lives, and, you know, she takes the pressure off by just offering, no questions asked. She'll say, "No, you go do what you need to do. Whether it's sleep or go for a training run. Like, we're here to help". I think that makes a huge difference.

My parents or even other parents of my kids' friends will even offer to take the kids for a play date – off my hands – so that I can go and train. Sometimes I would accept this offer, as it is so helpful. But then again, I could rarely reciprocate with full time work, training, and the kids. So, although I felt like this was amazing and kind, how could I ask these women who were also mothers and had time demands, to take my kids for two hours, just so I could go for a run or a bike or whatever? But, you know, if you're going to do sports, the truth is you really need the help and I'm not always good at asking for it or receiving it. I really am not. I guess the people who do have the success and dedicate themselves maybe either accept that help or they do what many women do, which is feel guilty about asking for it or taking it and continue with the 'juggling act'. It's funny because even as I say this, I know how important that support system is, but I still have trouble sometimes asking for it or receiving it.

Vignette 5: Killing Two Birds with One Stone

Once I got more involved with training after I had kids, like about a year or so into it, I realized that there were a lot of parents who do sport and are active with training goals. Maybe that community is in reality very small, but somehow, we all found each other. Like you go to races and after a while you start to notice that pretty much anyone over the age of 35 usually has kids there or in the background. It's actually the case for a lot of mums that are active maybe doing this to get their social time in along with the sport. Like, when you're so busy with working full time, and if you're training for things like triathlons, the way they get their social time in is training with a group of other girlfriends. This is a great way to get out of the house to spend time with a group of like-minded people, who are parents but also understand the rigours of training and the desire to reach sport performance goals. Something my husband and I noticed, particularly after our second child came along, was that we never see people socially as much for things like regular dinners or movies or whatever. So somehow along the way it evolved into most of our friends are either involved with sport like us with training, or we don't see those other people as much. Going to my swim group or running group, particularly at the weekends, where I meet other athlete parents, especially women, really helped me get much needed social time. This way too I didn't have to create more time in my schedule to be with other people and I still get the training in. I often have to get my training in alone due to scheduling with the family, but I find a few times a week or at the weekend, with others doing a lot of good for me and the family. Sometimes in the weekend groups, there are things for kids too, because everyone has kids in tow. We all have shared experiences sure, but it is just a great way to do what we love, which is sport, and connect with others through sport. It's really helped with my progress with my training, but also my mental health – like to be able to just talk and laugh with people or look forward to that group. There is something special about women coming together with sports being the commonality, because for most of us it was so much more than sports that brought us here in the first place.

Lately I've been picking races where there's more of a social component, so I texted my husband from this race I was at, and I said "I'm done coming to races by myself. Cuz it's just, it's not as fun". It's just… it's… it's too much of a focus on me, when I'm by myself. I really like the distraction of having other people around and it really feeds more of my need to connect with others. There's still a part of me that wants to see how I can perform and I'm competitive to set good times for my own goals, but that's not my main or only driver. When I do races by myself, I really feel that void. Moving forward, that's one of my biggest terms for selecting races – the social component. This kind of a mindset also fits with choosing races that the family can come along, for a longer stretch of time, to maybe be with friends.

Reciprocity of Motherhood and Sport

Vignette 6: Sport Is My Therapy and Home

Being an athlete makes me happy. It makes me feel more complete. It makes me a better parent in that sense because I am approaching my role as a parent feeling more complete, and in lots of different ways. For one thing, after my first child was born, at times I felt…I don't know…lost or maybe just not like myself or sort of not knowing if I would still have something for just me. So, it was very important to keep a bit of myself and, you know, be there for my children, but not just have 'me' be only about that. Of course, I would do anything for them and be any person that I need to be for them, but I didn't want to forget who I was as a person. Doing sport kind of helped me find myself again, and also keep uncovering different aspects of myself. It's for sure a 'happy place' and like a therapy, that does something good for me being this athlete, but also then as a mum. I hear some women talking about 'well mummy has her wine' and that's okay to destress with, good for them. For me being able to return to the trail, or the pool or whatever that is with my training time, gives me some of that regeneration, and also development time. It takes me out of the chaos or daily grind, but helps me also figure things out in a positive way. Doing sport – like being out on the trail or whatever – gives me serenity feeling like "This is my time. This is completely quiet. I don't have to answer to anybody. It's just me in the woods with no noise". So being an athlete balances me and I feel like I can be a much more patient mum as well. Cuz I have a therapy session out there. I have that session sometimes for two hours or even if it's 40 minutes of quiet time to myself and almost in a meditation state. Other times, it's being out there with others, and it helps me feel good that we are pushing each other to reach our goals.

When I get out there on the trail, there's a lot of reflection going on, so that's also part of the therapy. It's also very meditative for me to where sometimes I use it to get this connection with who I am, which transfers over to the family. Afterwards, I am more available as a parent. And being an athlete, it just brings in another dimension as to how I can be a positive role model. I've been appreciating this more and more over the last year, as I see my kids taking an interest in sport for themselves. If they don't want to do it that's okay, but they are showing an interest. So much of what I am learning about myself as an athlete, I'm seeing the parallels with other aspects of my life and with the kids. I am learning lessons from them about how I competed and how I handle that as an athlete cuz I come to it from a different place now. I think about this during my races often. Umm "What would I say to my kids right now?" Like when there's races when I'm feeling like "Oh my God, I wanna quit". I'm often going off through my mind, "What would I tell my kids right now if this was them?" and... and that has helped me. It's helped get me through or other times given me a sense of perspective with the race or how I could approach my training with more fun, not take it so seriously. Like I think about how carefree my son looks when he runs. When I start to feel really sluggish in my run, I'm like "Okay, be like my son. Be like him. He's a little reindeer, frolicking and light and enjoying it. Just be like him". Yea, sport is like home for me.

Reflective Questions

Keeping with the social constructionist narrative inquiry tradition in which our CNF vignettes are grounded, in closing this chapter, we offer five reflection questions for readers to think with, rather than about, the stories (Smith, 2016). These questions relate to deeper engagement with how these stories might resonate with readers' own lives in new, different, and/or parallel ways:

1   What stories do you react most 'strongly' to – positively and/or negatively – and how do those reactions relate to your own physical activity or sport experiences and goals?
2   What surprised you about these stories, and what did not surprise you about, the stories? Ponder why that might be.
3   In what ways do these stories reveal inclusion for some, but exclusion, for others?
4   What do these stories tell you about 'taken for granted' ideals that hold women responsible for making sport a part of their lives, without social or structural support?
5   What can also be learned about how these stories might lead to encouraging sport participation for mums?

References

Batey, J., & Owton, H. (2014). Team mums: Team sport experiences of athlete mothers. *Women in Sport and Physical Activity Journal, 22*(1), 20–36. https://doi.org/10.1123/wspaj.2014-0010

Braun, V., Clarke, V., & Weate, P. (2016). Using thematic analysis in sport and exercise research. In B. Smith & A. C. Sparkes (Eds.), *Routledge handbook of qualitative research in sport and exercise* (pp. 191–205). New York, NY: Routledge.

Carless, D., & Douglas, K. (2016) Narrating embodied experience: Sharing stories of trauma and recovery. *Sport, Education and Society, 21*(1), 47–61. doi:10.1080/13573322.2015.1066769

Frank, A. W. (2010). *Letting stories breathe: A socio-narratology.* Chicago, IL: University of Chicago Press.

McGannon, K. R., & Mauws, M. K. (2000). Discursive psychology: An alternative approach for studying adherence to exercise and physical activity. *Quest, 52*, 148–165. doi:org/10.1080/00336297.2000.10491707

McGannon, K. R., McMahon, J., & Gonsalves, C. A. (2017). Mother runners in the blogosphere: A discursive psychological analysis of online recreational athlete identities. *Psychology of Sport and Exercise, 28*, 125–135. doi:10.1016/j.psychsport.2016.11.002

McGannon, K. R., McMahon, J., & Gonsalves, C. A. (2018). Juggling motherhood and sport: A qualitative study of the negotiation of competitive recreational athlete mother identities. *Psychology of Sport and Exercise, 36*, 41–49. doi.org/10.1016/j.psychsport.2018.01.008

McGannon, K. R., & Schinke, R. J. (2013). "My first choice is to work out at work; then I don't feel bad about my kids": A discursive psychological analysis of motherhood and physical activity participation. *Psychology of Sport and Exercise, 14*, 179–188. doi.org/10.1016/j.psychsport.2012.10.001

McGannon, K. R., & Smith, B. (2015). Centralizing culture in cultural sport psychology research: The potential of narrative inquiry and discursive psychology. *Psychology of Sport and Exercise, 17*, 79–87. doi:10.1016/j. psychsport.2014.07.010

McMahon, J. (2016). Creative analytical practices. In B. Smith & A. C. Sparkes (Eds.), *International handbook of qualitative methods in sport and exercise* (pp. 302–315). New York, NY: Routledge.

Miller, Y. D., & Brown, W. J. (2005). Determinants of active leisure for women with young children—An "ethic of care" prevails. *Leisure Sciences, 27*, 405–420. doi:10.1080/01490400500227308.

Smith, B. (2016). Narrative analysis in sport and exercise: How can it be done? In B. Smith & A. Sparkes (Eds), *Routledge handbook of qualitative research in sport and exercise* (pp. 260–273). New York, NY: Routledge.

Smith, B., McGannon, K., & Williams, T. (2016). Ethnographic creative nonfiction: Exploring the what's, whys and how's. In G. Molnar & L. Purdy (Eds.), *Ethnographies in sport and exercise research.* London, UK: Routledge.

Smith, B., & Sparkes, A. C. (2016). Interviews: Qualitative interviewing in the sport and exercise sciences. In B. Smith & A. C. Sparkes (Eds.), *Routledge handbook of qualitative research in sport and exercise* (pp. 103–205). New York, NY: Routledge.

Spalding, N. J., & Phillips, T. (2007). Exploring the use of vignettes: From validity to trustworthiness. *Qualitative Health Research, 17*(7), 954–962. doi:10.1177/1049732307306187

Spowart, L., Burrows, L., & Shaw, S. (2010). I just eat, sleep and dream of surfing: When surfing meets motherhood. *Sport in Society, 13*, 1186–1203. doi:10.1080/17430431003780179

Vair, H. (2013). The discourse of balance: Balance of metaphor and ideology. *Canadian Review of Sociology, 50*, 154–177. doi:10.1111/cars.12010

5 'I'm Hurting but I'm Buzzing'

The Lived Experience of 'Positive Pain' in Competitive Swimming

Gareth McNarry, Adam B. Evans, and Jacquelyn Allen-Collinson

Introduction

In recent years, a growing corpus of sociological work has developed, drawing influence from existential phenomenology, and seeking to challenge taken-for-granted assumptions regarding the often underexplored, and 'mundane' elements of sporting experience. Pain is, all-too-often, one of those mundane elements of sports and 'serious' exercise participation. The ability to endure, ignore, or play through pain is commonplace in many physical and sporting cultures (Allen-Collinson, 2017), including competitive swimming (McNarry, Allen-Collinson, & Evans, 2020a, 2020b), distance running (Hockey & Allen-Collinson, 2016), triathlon (Bridel, 2010), and mountaineering (Allen-Collinson, Crust, & Swann, 2018), to give just some examples. Indeed, participants are often subjected to bodily pain that would not be acceptable or tolerated in other social situations (Bridel, 2010). Not only is pain tolerated, but certain types of pain have become normalised, even valorised, within certain physical cultures, so that an athlete's ability to endure pain and hardship is celebrated and worn as a badge of honour. Swimming is one such physical culture, and experiences of pain, along with other 'intense embodiment' (Allen-Collinson & Owton, 2015) experiences of training and competition, are core elements of participation. In this chapter, we focus more specifically on experiences of 'positive pain', drawing on data collected as part of a wider doctoral study conducted by Gareth. This ethnographic study employed a sociological-phenomenological theoretical approach to generate novel insights, and a richer and deeper understanding of the competitive swimming lifeworld, including how competitive swimmers must learn over time how to distinguish and interpret different types of pain. Furthermore, swimmers must develop specific coping strategies in order to make the pain 'actively absent', allowing them to 'shut it out' and continue to push their bodies to, and often beyond, their limits.

DOI: 10.4324/9781003038900-8

Ethnographic data were collected by the lead author, Gareth, from a group of competitive swimmers based at an English university, via overt participant observation (approximately 300 hours) and semi-structured interviews (12 male and 7 female swimmers) during three separate field 'immersions' spanning a full swimming season. During this time, Gareth adopted the role of a volunteer assistant, allowing him privileged access to this particular lifeworld. Fieldnotes were recorded on the OneNote iPhone application during each training session and subsequently written up as soon as possible afterwards. Semi-structured interviews were conducted, seeking to understand themes of the lived everyday world from participants' own perspectives. Swimmers were sampled for interview according to criteria that included being a member of a performance squad and having competed at a minimum of British Championship level in the previous 12 months. These inclusion criteria covered all members of the existing performance squads, so opportunistic sampling was then used in order to select a variety of athletes covering specialisms in different swimming strokes and events.

In total, 19 individual interviews (mean 75 minutes), spanning a range of experience from British Championship level through to athletes who had competed internationally at the World Championships and the Commonwealth Games, were conducted during field immersion one. Interviews were transcribed verbatim between immersion one and two. A follow-up interview was then held with each participant during immersion two, to seek clarification on points raised during the first interview. A final set of group interviews was then conducted during immersion three, allowing for further questions, critique, feedback, and collaboration as part of the data collection process. Thematic data analysis revealed a raft of lived experiences, including the salience of pain, which would often accompany the swimmers' day-to-day training routines. Discomfort and 'good pain' were portrayed by the swimmers as distinctive sensations that they came to understand as 'positive'. The data represented in the following creative nonfiction (CNF) are taken from our article entitled '"You always wanna be sore, because then you are seeing results": Exploring positive pain in competitive swimming' published in the *Sociology of Sport Journal* (McNarry, Allen-Collinson, & Evans, 2020b).

The original representation employed within both the thesis and the journal article followed a presentational style commensurate with the phenomenologically-sensitive aims of the sociological doctoral project. In order to generate the CNF, and taking up Gareth's idea for transforming the data, after discussion among all three authors, we decided to design the CNF to read like extracts from a competitive swimmer's training week. This would chart four different training sessions that swimmers would typically experience in a week in the water. The swimmers studied would regularly complete between seven and ten sessions in the pool per week, totalling on average between 30 and 70 km of swimming per week, but on occasion some might even complete up to and beyond 100 km. Added to this would be three to five land-based sessions that could (and often did) include weight training, 'Spin' classes, Pilates, or circuit training. Whilst Gareth was the primary instigator of our narrative, Adam and Jacquelyn contributed their own creative and analytic thoughts, and we all engaged in fascinating and enjoyable dialogue about the creative process as well as the narrative itself, as we added our own individual 'shapings' to the story, whilst seeking to remain 'true' to the voices of participants. The training week begins…

A Week Like Most Others on the Swimming Pain Train

Monday AM: The Weekly 'Wake Up'

Pre-Session

SHIIIIIIT, is it really Monday morning again? The weekends go way too quickly. The after-effects of last week's cruel increase in training-load are still pulling in my shoulders. This shift from our general preparation work, where we were only doing one session a day at low intensities and volume, to now doing some pretty fast stuff, has left me achy. It's sore just lying in bed this morning, and sitting down over the weekend was damn near impossible due to the tightness in my legs, back, and shoulders. I felt like I'd gone 12 rounds with Mike Tyson in his prime, as opposed to just swimming up and down a pool. It's a good ache, though: I'm getting fitter, stronger, and my technique is also improving. Hell, though, I'm just glad that Monday morning is a 'wake up' session because I've got an inkling I'll need something a bit softer and shorter to get me into the week. I lie, trying to wake up, eyes grainy, stubbornly shut. Then, biting the bullet, I crawl out of my warm bed into the cold darkness, fumbling around for clothes, choosing the warmest things I own, heading out to the pool through the dark, eerily quiet early-morning world.

The Session

At the pool, I enter via the automatic doors into the deserted reception area, stopping to fill my drinks bottle in preparation for the session. Proceeding through the glass doors, emblazoned with the message that challenges us to follow in the footsteps of those swimmers who have come before us, and it's into the brightly-lit pool area housing *our* eight-lane 50 m pool. It's not really *ours*, but this is how we refer to it, as this is where we spend most of our time. The air is warm but not stifling and there is the customary, very familiar hint of chlorine in the air, so redolent of indoor swimming. To others less accustomed to the sensorium of the swimming pool, this odour might be overpowering; to me, the smell and smelling of chlorine is just second nature. Meandering my way to my usual changing spot, I'm pissed to see someone else's stuff there. Their gear is quickly flung out of the way (as is usual practice) with an accompanying, proprietorial thought about which bell-end has put their stuff in my space! As I look around for culprits, I quickly glance up at the banners hanging at the end of the pool that depicts some of the success stories that our programme has had on the international swimming stage, and wonder if my name will one-day be among them. This is familiar territory; a second home, a place where I belong. Right now, though, my mind and body are complaining about the ludicrously early hour, and I see I'm not the only one still feeling a bit groggy. As my team-mates and I greet each other with grunts or yawns, it makes me feel that bit better about myself, knowing that they too are having a 'typical' Monday. As I change, I remember that I need my skipping rope from the bottom of my bag and have to go digging for it. I hate skipping on a Monday morning. I know why we do it, but at 5:15 in the morning the last thing I really want to be doing is jumping up and down.

I move to the end of the pool below the scoreboard where we begin our normal routine of skipping for 60 seconds and then stretching/mobilising various body parts for 60 seconds. Before we begin, there is an eerie air of stillness about the pool, with only the low hum of the pool itself creating any noise, as if it's still in its overnight slumber, breathing heavily. This silence is suddenly punctured by the echoing call of the coach, Nick: 'Right then, here we go, 2, 1, skip' and the whack, whack, whack, of skipping ropes slapping the tiles, as they are turned over and over and over. As I progress through this first 60 seconds, I can't help but check in once again with my body. As I jump, my legs feel leaden, shoulder muscles are tight and rigid, and I think to myself how I would love to be back in bed, tucked up under the nice warm duvet. Starting to mobilise areas of stiffness is like trying to stretch blocks of granite as opposed to muscles. I just feel sore and heavy everywhere. My thoughts begin to turn to the potential train wreck of a session that is to come. I feel like I'm not even going to be able to pull my arm through the water, let alone swim. But as we gradually move through the pre-pool routine, I begin to wake up. Coach Tony comes over to deliver the news of the training session we have in store this morning; "Ok people, nothing major or too shocking this morning. I know last week was tough, but this is a new week and we go again, starting with some gold and varied-pace". Thank God, it's fairly straightforward: speedwork (gold), followed by varied-pace aerobic work. Shouldn't be too much trouble or too taxing on the body, reckons

Tony. Just a way of 'rebooting the system'. Not sure I agree with Tony, and I mumble something to the effect of 'he obviously doesn't know how ropey I feel' to Frank next to me. I get a sarcastic 'amen' back.

Getting ready to get into the water on a Monday morning is always a struggle. I just stare at the water, seeing that it is *visibly* cold, its dark blue icy complexion just staring back at me, almost laughing at me as it laps over the end of the pool trying to reach forward and touch my toes. Others have already entered the water and started swimming. Their entry and subsequent movement through the water seems to have awoken the pool from its slumber. This invasion evokes a low grumble of displeasure that these human bodies have disturbed the blue tranquillity. I can almost sense the water's unease beginning to match mine as I prepare to dive in, anticipating the icy-water touch on skin, and the cold rushing throughout my body. But in I must get. So, it's a deep breath and a gentle, encouraging nudge from a team-mate to start the process of falling forward, before I push with the legs and enter a brief state of weightlessness as my body arcs through the air in my dive, arms squeezed either side of my head, toes pointed, and then…SHOCK!

As I connect with the water, I feel its cool embrace rush across my skin. I'm relieved that it's not freezing; that would have been another real ballache to add to my already worrisome bodily feeling. With eyes closed initially from the shock, I begin some hard 'dolphin' kicking[1] underwater, willing my body to adjust to the cold. As I open my eyes, I'm dimly aware of other bubbling, clear-white arrow-streaks appearing around me as other swimmers dive into the water and arc through it beneath the surface. Their black goggled-eyes above air-enclosed faces as they exhale underwater, doubtless experiencing a similar shock to my own. But my attention is on myself. Arm pulls, kick turns to a freestyle kick, and I rise from the subaquatic world into the layer between air and water. As I begin to surface and get into the first part of the warm-up, my stroke seems short, my hands are slipping through the water rather than connecting with it and holding on. My shoulders are grinding like an old millstone crushing grain, but thankfully the deeper into the warm-up I go, the easier things start to become; looser, freer, and closer to normal. But certainly not 'there' yet. That comes later. I *hope* it comes later!

The first block of this morning's 'main set' (not really a 'main set' in the traditional sense, as it's Monday morning), has us going 24 × 50 m repeats which we can do either butterfly or backstroke. I choose the backstroke option. I'm not sure my stiff and achy shoulders are ready for 1,200 m of butterfly, especially not on a Monday as I try to ease myself into the week. As I finish the first set of holding stroke rate 50s,[2] I look across at my co-swimmers, Remy and Wade. Remy moans 'oh God, my shoulders' and Wade replies in a mumbled matching groan. We all blow out our cheeks, sigh, and shake our heads in mutual (mock) despair. Between reps we are all rubbing our traps [trapezius muscles], massaging them out a little bit to loosen the painful knots that lurk right in their middle. But as soon as the clock gets back to our interval to go, it's off the wall and back into it for the next rep. It's automatic. Drop under the water, arm passes over-head, push hard, glide, KICK, breakout into the stroke and enjoy the light relief of the rest interval during the first few strokes before the numbness in the shoulders starts building again.

Post-Session

With the session done and dusted and the first 5 km of swimming over for the week, it's out and off to the shower to stand under the hot water for a few minutes before I contemplate getting changed and heading off to the gym for the first lifting session of the week. I stand, head lowered, just breathing for a moment. I'm conscious I am still breathing at the same rhythm as I would in the pool, so automatic are my embodied rhythms, but the pause is welcome. Not for long – the insistent, gnawing hunger pangs have begun. My thoughts are already turning towards getting home and gorging on breakfast. I'm always starving after our back-to-back swim/gym workout on a Monday morning. Thankfully I have no lectures today until 1 pm, so I know I'll be able to lift, get home, eat, and then get back into bed and sleep until lunchtime. I just hope my housemates haven't pilfered all the bread, cereal, and milk before I get home! Perhaps I'll pick up a spare loaf on the way home just in case, and park myself next to the toaster when I get in and just keep eating until I feel full. The record is 12 slices of toast, I wonder how many I'll get through today!

Tuesday PM – Anaerobic Endurance

Pre-Session

God, I hate Tuesdays! Morning training followed by a full day of lectures, so no nap and not enough food. Mental exhaustion assails me – from trying to concentrate for that long, as well as trying not to fall asleep. But it's no rest for the wicked until tonight's masterpiece is out of the way. Another two hours of training and Tuesday PM has been marked as a 'quality' session this week. I implicitly know it's gonna be a hurter! What it is, I don't yet know, but I just *know* it's gonna be rock hard, a real ordeal, a test of how I endure *that* pain, especially if I am feeling like I am. I'm just praying it's one of those days when I feel awful beforehand, but once I'm in the water it all washes away.

During pre-pool, I do my best to loosen up and help ease the DOMS[3] created after yesterday's swim/gym/swim, and from sitting in lectures all day, squashed into an old lecture theatre, where the seats have less legroom than a budget airline, listening to an old professor drone on about this and that. My attention strays to those *knots* in my muscles. These damned regular companions I carry around with me at all times in my arms, neck, and back, letting me know who and what I am. They need attention if I'm to cope with what lies ahead. As I go for the foam-roller, I look cross and Natasha, one of the sprinters, is just shaking her head, 'I feel grim tonight' she mouths across to me. Like her fellow sprinters, she has to endure an extra gym session on a Tuesday, so it's DOMS on top of DOMS for her and Co.

With one ear, I listen to her bang on about how sprinters have it so bloody much harder than the middle-distance or distance guys, as I slowly, gingerly, roll out my back, pausing at each vertebra just momentarily. It's then on to the old lats [Lattisimus Dorsi] and a bit of time on legs still sore from yesterday's squat session in the gym. With that bit of relief undertaken, Reed, our physio, then leads us through a mobility routine akin to some form of medieval torture. Still, by the end of the sequence, I'm starting to feel more swimmer, loose and fluid, than student, stiff and deskbound.

The Session

As we dive in, and work our way through the warm-up, I'm pleasantly surprised to find that my body feels 'ok', not great but not horrendous, and I'm able to hit and hold the paces needed to swim the main set at the right intensity and heart-rate, something that doesn't often happen as times and heart-rates can mysteriously fluctuate day by day! I'm therefore starting to feel slightly more positive about how tonight is going to go.

The set is a number of 100 m repeats working in a pattern of 1 easy (E), 1 best average[4] (BA), 1 E, 2 BA, 1 E, 3 BA, 1 E, 2 BA, 1 E, 3 BA, repeated twice for a total of 32. The first round of this isn't too bad. I can feel a bit of burn creeping in around the shoulders, lungs, and quads towards the end of the second set of 3 BA, but so far it's manageable. However, as I get to the last 10 reps, things are now a little different. As I enter the last 25 of each of the BA reps, it's really starting to hurt. Burning in my lungs, arms, and especially my quads. As I get to the wall, I can't even lift my head up to look up at the clock. The normal sounds of the pool are now punctuated by the sounds of heavy, laboured breathing, and the sensation of my heart beating in my head. It takes about 10 or 15 seconds for the numbness to start to recede. My muscles then start coming back to me and I begin to feel my arms, but suddenly, Wade, who is the person in front of me, pushes off for his next rep. I now have ten short seconds before it's my turn to go. As I push off the wall, the pain starts coming back and building once again. These back-to-back reps are the worst. It's only going to get worse and worse from here, but I'm swimming well so I'm just going to embrace this pain and try to keep going. It's nasty, it's grim, but I've accepted that I've reached a certain level of pain, good pain, and it can't get any worse. So I'm just going to keep smashing these reps until this fucking bitch of a set is over. I could ease off and there would be less pain, but then it's like, well, I've already reached my max, so what's the point in giving up. I yell at myself 'don't stop, keep fucking going, keep taking each rep as it comes'. It's fucking grim. It's fucking painful. But it's a good pain. That's just how it is. Masochist!

As we're finishing up, I catch Natasha's eye again as she sits shattered on the poolside, unable to move. 'Alright?' I ask, 'Buzzing', she replies, looking absolutely broken. 'I felt grim at the outset' she says, 'then a bit better through warm-up as it helped shift some of the lactate and soreness from the last 48 hours' training. However, I still started the main set, pretty much fucked, but sometimes, like tonight that's actually a good thing'. Pointing to her arms, she indicates really feeling the catch at the front of her stroke. It hurts when she gets it right, a kind of proper *feel* of the water. 'Being sore makes me feel stronger', she laughs. True. When you feel fresh, sometimes you just don't feel right.

Post-Session

Holy shit, I am *tired* and I am *hungry* after that session. After a luxuriant age in the shower, I just sit by my bag, towel around my shoulders, for what seems an eternity, waiting for the spirit to move me and I can begin to get changed. I can't even be bothered to stretch, I'm that tired... but I know I should. I just wish I'd brought something with me for a post-training snack. A schoolboy error, but I just wasn't expecting to be *this* hungry. It's a good sign though. It means when I go back to the house I can load up on pasta, meatballs, and sauce and then slump into a deep sleep without the threat of the early-morning alarm – Wednesday's session is at lunchtime!

Thursday PM – Aerobic Kick

Pre-Session

Thursday evening always throws up a quandary for me. On one hand, relief we've been out of the water since Wednesday afternoon and have had a chance to recover a little bit mid-week (still have a gym session Thursday AM, mind, but I'm talking swim here). On the other hand, it's often a kick-set and I hate kick-sets. I have never been what I would class as 'good at kick'. I'm not bad compared to the average swimmer but I'm rubbish compared to the majority of my team-mates. I fully expect this evening to be just another one of those days where I feel like I'm drowning at the back of the lane!

The Session

It's taken us ages to get in tonight, which only delays the inevitable death-session, but coaches Tony and Nick had some stuff they wanted to discuss with us before we got going. They are pissed that some guys missed our Pilates session yesterday afternoon as they were watching the rugby and forgot the time. It's never nice having these discussions, especially when you're not at fault; always makes me feel a bit awkward. With discussion over, it's on with hats and goggles: into our big blue friend we go for another two hours of 'getting better'. Working our way through the warm-up, I can't decide if it's simply mind-numbingly boring or I'm just not engaged because I'm not looking forward to the fiendishness Tony has designed for tonight's kick-set. I'm sure he was in a bloody bad mood when he wrote this session! Despite this, there's a glimmer of hope for me: as the warm-up ends, and against all the odds, my legs actually feel good to go, with only minor stiffness in my quads and hip flexors.

As we gather ourselves, Tony explains the set one more time. He must sense our apprehension as he keeps using phrases like 'challenge yourself', 'work with the person beside you', or 'be brave' to try and motivate and lift our mood. Despite this I take up my usual position at the back of the lane for kick. However, it becomes evident after the first few reps, that I'm *on one* tonight. I start to move up powerfully through the lane as each rep goes by, using those in front as unsuspecting targets to hunt down during each repetition. As the set carries on, there are rumblings from co-sufferers along the lines of: 'fucking hell, my legs' or 'come on legs', indicating they are starting to feel the effects. Normally I would be in the same boat, my legs would have likely given up a long time ago. But not tonight. Because I'm having such a good session, even more so as it's a kick-set, I've almost forgotten how much pain I'm in. I'm in the zone. I feel like I've turned into a different person, I'm operating in overdrive, the adrenaline and the endorphins are together carrying me through. I'm hurting, but I'm buzzing, so I just keep pushing on. Although my legs are a combination of being on fire in the quads and numb everywhere else, strangely, mysteriously, I have found a way to 'shut out the pain', 'forget about it', make it 'actively absent'. I keep pushing this newfound body through the final round.

This isn't always the case though (if only it were) especially in kick-sets. I'm not sure if it's some weird body thing, because the legs are at the opposite end to where your brain is and the signals don't quite get through. Sometimes it can be so damned frustrating because you want your legs to go at a certain pace, but then you hit a grim level of pain and they just don't listen. It's at this stage when I might objectify the bastards, shouting at them to 'come on'… but they don't have ears, so they never listen.

Post-Session

I'm changing and stretching off, chatting to Jessica, whose breaststroke group has just done a different set from mine. 'Like you get to 25[meters]', she says, 'and it just burns, like everything's burning, you start to get out of breath… my muscles start to ache and I'm fucking dying, desperate to stop. I just focus on my breathing, it helps me forget the sheer wall of pain. With breaststroke I go under and I just breathe everything out, come up, take a big, big breath and then, cos obviously I'm lucky with breaststroke, we can breathe every stroke, it's not like you guys with front-crawl – like, I'd be well rubbish at that'. She rolls her eyes and grins widely. 'Like, I take these big breaths and then just blow out everything and then just try and focus on being long and STRONG'. We agree, though: we are absolutely bollocksed, totally drained, but feeling good about things this evening. Well, maybe not *everything* as we're back in the pool in under 12 hours. I'll need the triple alarm for tomorrow morning to make sure I'm not late. Otherwise, I'll be experiencing a different type of pain: Nick and Tony would dish out some serious shit for missing a session especially after rollocking us earlier about people missing Pilates. Plus, I'd be utterly embarrassed that I'd let my team-mates down.

Saturday AM: Race Pace

Pre-Session

The alarms go off. I just lie, staring at the ceiling for a few moments. In denial. Finally, with a superhuman effort, I peel myself off the pillow, then the mattress, with a long, slow groan. If I didn't know it was Saturday morning already, my body would certainly tell me just by the way it feels. I ache top-to-bottom. Thank God it's the last session of the week, number 9 of 9 in the pool, with 5 of 5 land-training workouts also completed. It hasn't been pretty, but it's been fun in a weird sort of way. Not in the sense of actively seeking out this pain but accepting that it's just a normal part of our sport. This is what we swimmers do.

The Session

I arrive at the pool, get changed, and begin my pre-pool in a vain attempt to mobilise my body. Nick explains the set, then magnanimously offers: 'You've all got the option of doing MY lovely warm-up, guys, or doing your own, so long as you're suited-up (racing suits on) ready to go for the main set by 6:45am on the button!'. I decide to do my own thing; that way I can control the narrative and ensure I get myself prepared for what lies ahead.

Before beginning our main sets, we reorganise into different lanes depending on our set. As I gather my stuff and head towards lane 8, I can't help but notice the looks of gnawing concern and deep apprehension written all over Eddie's and Stephen's faces. It's strangely comforting as it dawns on me they're feeling just as apprehensive about this set as I am. We all exchange looks that silently convey between us the thought of just how much this going to hurt!!!

It doesn't take long to find out. On the first of the 15 m underwater reps, coming back up to the surface, I literally have to bark the air out of my lungs and gulp in fresh oxygen; I genuinely felt like I wasn't going to make that, and it was only 15 m. The burning in my lungs and the desire to breathe while still underwater was like nothing I've ever experienced, and I've been doing this a l-o-n-g time. Holy shit, I've got another three rounds of this to go. I'm not going to make it… Then I see my team-mates on the side, one's already done this, one's yet to go. I know I can't let them down. Doing my best to compose myself between each rep and give each my best effort, I try desperately to ignore the lactate-burn building in my legs, or the bizarre desire of my lungs to breathe underwater. I focus on pushing through.

Finishing the last of the nine 50s, I'm out on to the side of the pool as quickly as I can be, starfish-sprawled on my back. My face is burning and all screwed up. My chest is heaving up and down as air rushes in and out of my lungs and I try to normalise my breath. My heart's pounding violently, pumping freshly oxygenated blood around my body. But more than anything I just feel numb. I don't even notice that Hank is trying to take a lactate reading from me. Once he's done I'm free to move around a little and begin shaking out arms and legs. At this point Scott comes over, gives me a look of concern, taps my shoulders and asks me if I'm 'ok hun?'. I just look up at him from my sprawled-out position, unable to respond properly, staring right through him in a way that I hope conveys: 'what do *you* think mate'.

Finally beginning to return to some sort of normality, I'm just about able to pick myself up from the floor, and decide to go for a walk to the opposite end of the pool. Trying to move, I'm drunkenly unsteady on my feet, legs jelly-like and unable to support me. I decide I need to sit down again and just compose myself a little more. As I sit, with elbows on knees, head hanging low, I start to feel the buzz of having just worked through a set of that magnitude. Beginning to feel better, I head back up towards the starting end where Eddie and Wade stand waiting. Nick comes over to ask how it was, and all I can reply with is, 'fucking hard. I was absolutely on my arse after the butterfly and it just got worse from there. I could hardly even make the underwaters'. Nick, being Nick, just smiles at me, like he does, and says 'good, that's what we wanted'. Smiling inwardly, I think 'you bastard'.

Post-Session

I. AM. DONE! I couldn't have given any more to that session than I did. Absolutely disgusting while doing it. My arms felt like they both weighed 100 kilos and my technique was all over the place towards the end, both of which were horrible to try and push through. But now that the set, the session, and the week are over, there's the grim satisfaction of knowing it's all about suffering to improve. Because when you're absolutely dead, but you push yourself through that, then you know, that's one step closer to a PB (personal best).

Finale

This week has been brutal. I've had times where I've questioned what the hell I'm doing here, smashing my body up and down a pool, but I just love it. I think I love it because there's no pressure on me at this point. I feel awful, but there is no pressure to do amazing, it's about pushing myself and giving what I can give. But if I can swim as well as I have this week when I'm feeling shit, then I'm excited to see what I can do when I've had some rest and I'm feeling good. Here's to a season of potentially great or even spectacular things.

So yeah, I guess being sore is a good thing. Maybe you always wanna be sore because then you are seeing results? If I was always just feeling easy and everything was always easy then everyone would be able to do it. But if you're feeling sore and you're seeing results, then in season, the sorer and heavier I feel, the better.

Reflective Questions

1   In what way does this CNF resonate with the experiences of pain in your sport or physical-cultural lifeworld?
2   Does your sport or physical culture have similar (or indeed different) categories of pain?
3   How would you describe the different forms of pain (and their positive, negative, or productive characteristics) in your sport/physical culture to a nonparticipant?
4   Might there be negative aspects to a sporting mind-set and culture that valorise and prize 'good' pain?

Notes

1 Dolphin Kicking is an action often used by swimmers to travel underwater. The arms remain in a streamline position with the legs performing a simultaneous up and down action, like the tail of a dolphin.

2   50s refers to 50 m swimming repeats, and stroke rate refers to the number of
    arm rotations that a swimmer takes per minute of swimming.
3   Delayed Onset of Muscle Soreness.
4   In a best average set swimmer's aim is to hold the best average time they
    could across the whole set. The aim is to be fast but consistent.

References

Allen-Collinson, J. (2017). Injured, pained and disrupted bodies. In M. Silk, D.
    L. Andrews, & H. Thorpe (Eds.), *Routledge handbook of physical cultural stud-
    ies* (pp. 267–276). London: Routledge.
Allen-Collinson, J., Crust, L., & Swann, C. (2018). 'Endurance work': Embodiment
    and the mind-body nexus in the physical culture of high-altitude mountaineer-
    ing. *Sociology, 52*(6), 1324–1341. https://doi.org/10.1177/0038038517746050
Allen-Collinson, J., & Owton, H. (2015). Intense embodiment: Senses of heat
    in women's running and boxing. *Body & Society, 21*(2), 245–268. https://doi.
    org/10.1177/1357034X14538849
Bridel, W. F. (2010). *"Finish…whatever it take" considering pain and pleasure in
    the ironman triathlon: A socio-cultural analysis* (Unpublished doctoral disser-
    tation). Queen's University, Kingston, Ontario, Canada.
Hockey, J., & Allen-Collinson, J. (2016). Digging in. The sociological phenom-
    enology of "doing endurance" in distance running. In W. Bridel, P. Markula,
    & J. Denison (Eds.), *Endurance running. A socio-cultural examination* (pp.
    227–242). London: Routledge.
McNarry, G., Allen-Collinson, J., & Evans, A. B. (2020a). 'Doing' compet-
    itive swimming: Exploring the skilled practices of the competitive swim-
    ming lifeworld. *International Review for the Sociology of Sport.* https://doi.
    org/10.1177/1012690219894939
McNarry, G., Allen-Collinson, J., & Evans, A. B. (2020b). "You always wanna be
    sore, because then you are seeing results": Exploring positive pain in compet-
    itive swimming. *Sociology of Sport Journal, 37*(4), 1–9. https://doi.org/10.1123/
    ssj.2019-0133

6   The Backstage of 'Seeing' Performance

Developing the 'Seen' and 'Unseen' of Coaching

Charles L. T. Corsby

Introduction

The research study which gave life to this chapter was a ten-month ethno-methodologically informed ethnography of a semi-professional football club. The wider aim of the study was to deconstruct contextual actors' interactions, paying specific attention to the conditions under which such behaviours occur, that is, how the members in the setting were able to produce, manage and manipulate interactions and context to improve learning and influence. The project was inspired by the writings of Harold Garfinkel, whose work coalesced into ethnomethodology. Adhering to ethnomethodology's uncompromising commitment to observe the details of ordinary society, the primary research method adopted was participant observation. More specifically, I was positioned in the field as a player within the club in question, an involvement that has outgrown the initial research. Such a claim follows Lynch's (1993) requirement of 'unique adequacy,' that is, the disciplinary specialities (i.e., coaching) can only be studied by "getting inside" the relevant practices (p. 276). In this respect, I, as the researcher, claim such a standing as a competent practitioner within the setting (in addition to a much longer history in other football clubs).

The fuller methodological discussion and subsequent findings from the project can be found in Corsby and Jones (2019a, 'Observation, evaluation and coaching: the local orderliness of "seeing" performance'; 2019b, 'Complicity, performance, and the "doing" of sports coaching: An ethnomethodological study of work'). However, despite the assertion of 'being there,' I do not claim a privileged right to unproblematically speak for those under study. Rather, in line with the work's interpretivist grounding, I accept that my interpretations and sense-making of the dataset are partial and fragmented (Sparkes, 2002). The aim of this chapter, then, drawing upon creative nonfiction, is to reconsider, refashion and, in parts, re-analyse the previous 'realist' representation of the results. However, rather than attempting to provide a 'good' literary tale, the significance of this endeavour lies in highlighting the contextual specificity

DOI: 10.4324/9781003038900-9

of the analysis previously presented. In doing so, the purpose is not only to creatively complement the existing analysis presented in Corsby and Jones (2019a, 2019b), but rather, I attempt to elevate the reflexive and confessional features of the original study by illustrating the various 'back stages' of coaching. In this way, while the stories presented are grounded by the original dataset found in Corsby and Jones (2019a, 2019b), the creative features involved recasting the experiences of the characters embedded in the context to capture subtleties of time, location and setting. This is not an attempt to replace the original realist accounts, but to use my personal confessions as a way of capturing the nervous 'looseness' and 'openness' of the fieldwork undertaken (Van Maanen, 1988). This shift in representation towards confessional tales attempts to spark interest in the 'unseen' and often ignored backstage of athletes while subject to being 'seen,' of which, builds upon the predominant analysis offered in Corsby and Jones (2019a, 2019b). As a result, the creative nonfiction story takes the form of a series of interrelated diary extracts adapted from the original fieldnotes and reflexive journal. While some features have been developed for the purpose of this chapter, the positionality of these stories reflects the original design of the ethnographic project.

This project contributes to the growing body of literature within sports coaching, specifically studies which have wrestled with the endemic complexity and pathos of coaching (e.g., Jones, 2006, 2009; Potrac, Jones, Gilbourne, & Nelson, 2012). Within this growing corpus of research, coaching is placed as an inherently relational and pedagogical activity (e.g., Jones, Edwards, & Viotto Filho, 2014), which requires coaches to manage the emotionality and performativity of their roles. More recently, such work has considered the everyday micro-realities of coaches 'doing' this important 'work' (e.g., Cronin & Armour, 2015; Gale, Ives, Potrac, & Nelson, 2019; Corsby & Jones, 2019b). At the heart of this contribution, then, is the desire to provide a further nuanced reading of sports coaches' (and athletes') work by illuminating the interpersonal connections between coach, athletes and context. It is hoped that such inquiry, in its developed representation, has much to offer not only researchers in field (and wider), but also generates rich insights into the coaches, athletes and educators 'on-the-ground.' Following the extracts, a series of reflective questions are presented for coaches, athletes and sport science practitioners more generally to consider.

The Everydayness of Football

Diary Extract, 1st July, Pre-Season Day 1

The first session of pre-season. Greens all the way; the car journey to the ground is smooth. The radio blasts the perfect sing-along for football, Queen. I glance at my watch while the tyres crunch across the car park,

18.45, plenty of time. One last check of my hair in the rear-view mirror. I am ready. I throw my wash bag under one arm; it contains only the essentials. Boots in one hand, keys dangling in the other. The beaten-up Ford next to me reflects my sidelights as the car locks; I don't look back.

I push the door back and hit an outstretched leg, '*Sorry mate.*' Bags fill the floor. Bayside's dressing room is like a warm bath; I feel comfortable. There's an awkward looking boy in the corner, I don't recognise him. Unfamiliar eyes harass me, adrenaline seeps into my stomach. The room vibrates with a hum of chatter. I find a seat on the far side and try to look relaxed, legs spread. The players sit quietly displaying various club emblems on their chest; an old version of Bayside's badge is on mine. Two players slumped in the corner discuss their previous clubs and friends in common. One reckons he had a pro; he looks young.

More players arrive, "*Char! Yes Char! Welcome back, son. How are ya?*" Woody bellows across the room. A smile fills my face. Woody strolls past the others. I notice his pristine white socks exaggerate his colourful trainers. A few stare. A moment passes in idle chatter before Rhys soon joins us, "*Who are these lot?*" he asks pointing his thumb towards his chest. "*Where is everyone? Where's James? I haven't spoken to him all summer... Guessing he ain't coming back. What about Richard? Clive? I thought more would be here,*" Rhys continues. Woody, now sitting on the bench, leans over to adjust his boots, "*James' gone Southside. Apparently, they got a new owner; more cash. Richard and Clive will be late, as usual,*" Woody replies. Rhys shakes his head.

Mark inflicts silence on his arrival. He looks in charge, scans the room and continues past the queue of players towards the awkward boy. "*Nice to meet you Will,*" offering his hand. Everyone stares at Will. Half standing-up, Will returns the handshake nodding, "*Thank you, Mark,*" before returning to his seat. Mark quickly turns to acknowledge Rhys and Woody before demanding, "*Waters' done!*" Within moments, Mark leaves and the players start to disperse. The dull noise of chatter resumes, I overhear the two players in the corner discuss Mark's previous professional career, "*Played in the Prem' he has.*"

Diary Extract, 3rd July: 'Best 11'

This week's return was smooth enough. After 18 months, I thought it would be tough returning to the club. I thought I'd be nervous. But I am not the same person, or the same player. I'm not some 'newbie' or some ex-youth scholar. "*I'm glad you are back,*" Mark said when he first saw me at the training ground. Mark always looked me in the eye when he shook my hand; his hand engulfed mine. Towering over me, "*How's the family, work? Dogs OK?*" he asked. Ben was the same; he always gave warm receptions. *"Great to see you buddy! Eh, don't mind this belly son. I've been working on it all summer,"* Ben says bursting into laughter. Smaller and stockier than Mark, he was protective of the younger players. Football never seemed as harsh when Ben was there. I was a beneficiary of that protection; I should have been more appreciative the first-time round. Not all the faces were the same, but it was good to work with Mark and Ben again.

The building, although weathered and worn, was rich with history and memories. Photos of previous year's teams scattered the corridor. Callum caught me staring, *"Are you fit?"* he barked, ushering me into the dressing room. *"I feel good, actually."* He nodded without breaking stride – 'actually' reverberated around my thoughts. I familiarised myself with names, face and, of course, boots. Alex; long blonde fringe and pink Nikes. Check. Freddie; piercing blues eyes and fluorescent Nikes. Check. Alfie; shaved head and black Adidas. Check. Callum even saved me a locker in the changing room; he told me later that he kept it from one of the *"young'uns."* Why did I say 'actually'? The manager phoned me, remember; he respected me. *"I'll get you back playing,"* Mark told me. The changing room was spacious. Eight of the lockers had numbers over the top. Callum's read '7'; a good number. The rest of the lockers had their numbers removed; my old locker was blank. No time for doubts – actually – Mark knows what I can do from the first-time round. It was unnerving having all the players direct their gaze at me in the dressing room, but I know the question, am I 'actually' in the best 11? That was Mark's requirement. That has always been the aim. That is what I need to do; I need to play well!

Diary Extract, 12th September: Match-Day 3

Mark calls Woody outside. Everyone knows but nobody looks. Woody returns head down. Back in his seat, he whispers to Rhys, *"Not starting mate. I fucking knew it. I'm fuming, can't be arsed to sit on the bench again. They reckon Mo will stretch the game better against this lot today."* I have been there before. Exposed. Lonely. Rejected. Rhys pauses, raising his eyebrows and sighs, *"What did you say?"* he asks. Woody replies, *"Nothing."* Rhys responds, *"That's tough on you man, you've done well recently. One of those things mate; stay sharp, you'll get on and you'll have to show they got it wrong."* He stands to adjust his socks, sincere but preoccupied.

Diary Extract, 14th September: 'Don't Be Late'

The players form groups of four and five with a ball except for Richard and Clive who stand laughing with Mark. Mark then turns to the clock overshadowing the pitch, *19.35.* *"Rhys"* he barks, *"Where is Phil?"* Rhys shrugs. *"Go for a run,"* he replies. Mark pulls out his phone as the players congregate and begin a lap of the pitch in silence. *"Where is he?"* Rhys mutters to Woody. Staring at his boots, Woody shakes his head.

Moments later Mark calls out for the group to reconvene. The players circle around the coaches, *"I'm preaching to the converted here, but I'm not having this. Phil is late again, he was late to the game, no phone call, no text, anyone know where he is?"* Mark begins. The players remain silent, staring at the floor. *"Well, I'm telling you, one of you needs to get a grip of him. I've had enough of this; he is late every week, and it is simply not good enough. I'm not late, Ben isn't late, everyone can make it on time, why can't he? It doesn't stop at lateness. You accept that, you accept a man running off his shoulder; you let him get away with it and won't say anything. I'm not having it. Off you go, do another lap and then we are back in."* The players leave. *"He is always late in fairness,"* Will mumbles. *"Keep it positive, lads. No moaning like fuck; you know Mark can sense it,"* said Richard.

Training finishes with set-pieces. Ben stands on the edge of the box. He takes one glance at the paper folded in his hand and begins to dictate where every player should be, *"Callum here… Alex, you need to be here."* The explanation unfolds and Ben shouts to Seb, *"Put it where we said, just lift it."* Seb plays his first corner over the heads of everyone. The on-rushing players provide a collective groan. Mark interludes, *"Try curling it Seb, just a bit of whip to the front post."* Seb follows Mark's instructions. Ben stands in silence. Seb's efforts are better but, by Ben's expression, the corner does not reflect what is scribbled on the paper. He glances one more time, *"No, not for me that, I think you should just lift it. Worse players than you can do this, come on Seb. Strike through it to the front post."* Seb, beginning to look more dejected, tries another corner. No success, again. Mark calls out, *"the curled corner worked better."* Ben strides over to Seb. He demands all the players' attention, *"Look… These corners really do work, they just require execution. This corner can be the difference and has been the difference between winning and losing a game. I'm telling you now, set plays are the way a lower league opposition can beat a higher standard opponent. All we need is one of these to work in a game and that is the difference of one point and three. Now it is all on the ball in Seb, just lift the ball to the front post"*.

He shadows the technique of striking a ball. Ben's usually calm demeanour evades him. Mark nods, he does not add to Ben's comments. *"We'll come back to this; maybe someone else can do it. 11 v 11, let's go,"* the players disperse.

The ball starts moving from side to side. Immediately, Callum springs towards Will. Will's hesitation allows Callum to whip the ball from his feet. Mark instantly barks from the side-line at the 'slow' ball movement. *"Why are you taking three, four touches there?"* Mark walks straight past me towards Will, *"You don't need to. Get your head up with a positive first touch and play into Tom or Phil. Two options minimum you have. If you two can't move the ball from the back then there is no point us playing. When we go away from quick ball movement and playing from the back we are average at best. I'd get 11 lumps if we were to shell it. Now move the ball quickly."*

Will looks bemused; he glances to Rhys for assurance before strolling back to his position.

I get back to the car with Will and Rhys; radio off and windscreen wipers on full. I usually drive; I don't have to speak when I drive... or pick the music. They won't like what I have to say; they look fatigued and frustrated. *"Mark doesn't give us a fucking break, does he?"* Will begins. Rhys continues, *"Yeah right, a few mistakes and the world's collapsed. I'm a defender and I get the most ball, I think he needs to see what else we are doing."* Will nods, *"We have the best defensive record in the league, does that not matter? I know I am not technically gifted, but he doesn't see that. Mind you, Seb couldn't hit a barn door tonight,"* We all laugh. *"That's true. Come on lads, we are a couple of ball playing centre halves. What's your thought on Saturday? Do you think Woody will be back in?"* Rhys asks. *"Will he fuck,"* Will answers. Rhys continues, *"He's done alright recently,"* Will is in the back, staring out the window, *"Yeah he started that game after Christmas and wasn't shit. He had a chance then, not sure Saturday is the time for a second,"* he responds. We catch eyes in the rear-view mirror; he looks tired and frustrated. A moment of silence follows. I pull into a layby to drop Will off. *"He never does much against Crittendale,"* Will mumbles stepping out of the car.

Diary Extract, 10th October: The 'Blues'

Another good win today; another good afternoon's work. We had the big coach travelling back too. Mercedes badges on each seat. I got my usual seat. I saw another article on Twitter about the 'blues': *'Blues extend their lead at the top.'* I hate the blues. We play them in two weeks, I can't wait! Mark asked me what was wrong with Woody. He barely spoke today; drove himself to the game. I'll text him: *Hi mate, I know you're frustrated at the moment, but your time will come. Keep your head up. Hope everything else is Ok at home.*

Diary Extract, 1st November: The Green Grass of Bayside F.C.

Mark sits opposite Ben, blue pen in one hand, piece of paper in the other. He starts to scribble names down on the paper. He pauses for a moment, sips his coffee and then continues to scribble names. He then slides the paper over to Ben and points to Callum's name, *"Callum is the one... [Short pause] When he is on his game, he gets goals and he is great, but* when he isn't, we might as well play with ten. Alex has to do his running for him. Laziest man I know,"

Mark waits for a response. "*I think you are being a bit harsh on him there. I think he looks much lazier than he is… He offers more than what we see. I do think he is trying,*" Ben replies. Mark becomes more defensive, "*He is, and I agree, I'm not saying that, but it's not enough. If only he would run a bit more, more proactive than reactive. How hard is it to run in behind? We would then have some player on our hands*".

Ben reaches for his coffee nods his head. "*I want to work on that pattern we discussed last week. I'll try Callum out in the patterns. Drink up, I want to be early for training,*" Mark gathers his bag, pulls on his bobble hat with the Bayside emblem printed on the front, and then begins to fasten up his coat. Mark is head to toe in Bayside's navy colours.

I arrive early at training and meet Mark by the pitch prior to training. We begin discussing some tactics regarding the team we are playing Saturday. "*We've got to get in behind them,*" he adds. I remind him of the gangly striker they have. He is relaxed. The tempo of his movement is slower compared to when the whole squad are there. I follow Mark while he methodically places cones. "*Me and Ben work together. I have known him for a while; he knows his stuff when it comes to football. I used to ask him what he thought of us [Bayside] whenever he came and watched. Then, about 3 years ago he joined as the assistant. He is great tactically, thinks about the game in different ways. He has also been around the level [of Bayside] a lot more than me, so he knows what the players are like and the struggles we have, like Saturday*".

We both smile. Mark continues, "*We can then bounce ideas off each other. I'll give you an example: ever since I started coaching, I always watch the games on the left corner of the box (technical area for coaches) and Ben will sit. I like being on my own in the box. We won't speak to each other through the game, maybe a few words, then if I see something happening that needs changing, I can ask him or we usually have a quick chat before the players come in (for half-time). Saturday for example, we weren't getting the ball out the back very well and we both agreed just before we said our piece to the players at half-time. It helps so we can support what we are saying.*"

Mark goes on to explain the exercises he has planned for the training session ahead. Mark's explanation is full of detail; he knows his stuff. "*Got to get Callum into these patterns,*" he adds.

Mark demands that Callum must move from his original spot for the pattern-of-play work. Callum nods and slowly moves in accordance with Mark's instruction whispering under his breath, "*Never works anyway.*" "*Let's try it again,*" Mark calls. Despite Mark's insistence, the players involved begrudgingly initiate the pattern again. After the session, I walk back to dressing rooms with Callum and Rhys. Callum expresses his frustration, *"Those patterns never work; I think they are shit. How many times they come out in a game? That ball behind is so hard to get on the end of. He shouts if I don't make it but half the time I have no chance".*

Rhys laughs, *"We don't score many, do we? I reckon just stick in there and see what happens. It's not personal, mate"* he replies.

Diary Extract, 3rd December: Seeing Red

The rain lashes down on the roof of the dressing room. At half-time Bayside are tied 1-1 in a derby with a local team. I feel good; a few tackles; a few passes. The second half gets underway and I win a free kick, which we convert. *2-1.* I've contributed. We reset with 30 minutes left. My heart pumps in my neck. *"Get the ball back; you've got to get the ball back,"* I whisper under my breath… [BANG] I fly into a tackle. The whistle blows. *"No way! That wasn't a foul."* The opposing player grabs and spins the ball out in front. A quick free kick and we are in trouble. I spring to the right to stop the play. The whistle blows again. I already have a yellow card. I'm in trouble. *"Sorry ref,"* I hold my hands up. He shakes his head; ex-copper. *"No chance I could get out the way,"* I plead. I hear the screams from the opposition bench. He shakes his head again, *"You stuck your leg out, you're gone."* He reaches for a yellow card before sliding a red one from his back pocket. His arm casts a shadow over my head. I scuttle to the bench. The crowd triples in size. Mark glares at me, *"Don't you fucking dare come here; you're not welcome!"* His words cripple me. The crowd taunts me. Guilt rushes through my stomach, what have I done?

I watched the remainder of the game peering from the side of the stand. Full-time. *3-1* win. They had done it. The players hug and smile; I dare not get too close. The fence around the pitch separates me from the team. Mark is blunt, *"Huge well done, we will chat inside."* The players leave and before long only Ben is left in the dug-out. He walks past me. He knows; I know. I stare at the floor, but he grabs my head and pulls it up. *"It's happened. Take your punishment and learn from it,"* he whispers and quickly catches up with the others.

I scarper back to the dressing room. The players are waiting. My seat is taken; I'll sit in the corner for now. Clive comes and sits next to me, he puts his arm around my shoulder *"I'll take the blame mate, I shouted stand on it,"* he says. My eyes raise. *"No, seriously, Mark went mad at me on the side-line for saying it. Blaming me for the incident."* I pause for a moment looking at him, *"I'm off the hook then."* Clive bursts into laughter. Mark enters, silence resumes, *"Fantastic performance today and a fantastic result. The way we defended with 10 men was fantastic, the application and commitment. I can't fault you… [long pause] If there is one sour note, and there is,"* Mark pauses and stares at me, *"Charlie, I could dock you a week's wages for today, downright stupid what you did out there. I thought you were supposed to be a bright; you need to thank your teammates tonight because they got you out the shit… You owe us."* I nod in agreement. He leaves with Ben by his side.

A pile of kits emerges on the floor. I start to fold the shirts into some order; numbers facing up. Seb taps me on his way to the shower, *"Mark was a bit harsh on you there,"* he says leaning into me, *"he didn't have to do that in front of everyone."* I return half a smile and continue folding. Seb is privy to a berating from Mark; he has been on the end of a few.

Diary Extract, 12th January: The Training Squad

Mark stops the passing drill to address one of the groups. I watch closely as he offers a demonstration of the movement; meanwhile Hamish shuffles towards Richard in the queue formed behind me. He whispers to Richard, *"Mate, fed up with this, I reckon we should split from the youth players. The quality in the session is shit. What do you reckon? Think we should say something?"* Richard nods, *"I agree mate, we can't string two passes together at the moment,"* he replies. Their noise makes me feel uncomfortable; what if Mark hears?

Richard strides towards Ben in-between the transition of drills, *"Ben, I think we should consider splitting the groups* [U23s players and 'senior' players] *up so we can raise the quality… You know, keep the quality. Like, make sure those who aren't sure, just keep everyone happy."* Ben winces at the comment. He takes a deep breath and strolls over to Mark, who was preparing the next exercise. Instantly, Mark shakes his head and calls for the attention of the group. Addressing everyone, Mark begins, *"Who isn't happy? If you don't want to stay, you can leave now! We've got a transfer window. I'm not interested in keeping people happy!"* Mark looks infuriated; Ben stands behind, arms folded. Hamish is on the edge of the circle to my left, while Richard is in front of me, directly in the middle of Mark's view. *"If any of you have an issue with the way things are being run, I suggest you speak now! I will justify my actions to any one of you and if you don't want to stay, you can leave. Apparently Richard has mentioned some of you think we should split the group up, does anyone have anything to add?… [Long pause] Hamish, anything?"*

Mark glares to his right at Hamish. Hamish shuffles his feet side-to-side staring at the floor, *"Urmm, I get that it isn't easy to split the groups."* Richard knows what is coming and quickly interrupts, *"Well,"* Mark's eyes dart back to the middle, *"I just mentioned it to raise the quality…"* Richard goes to speak again before Ben interrupts. He steps next to Mark to respond, *"Come on lads, whatever standard you play at, there will be differences. We are in this together. We are trying to improve."* Hamish nods and adds, *"I guess we need to raise the quality amongst ourselves lads, we all started at some place. Pull together eh lads... Yeah?"* Ben nods, *"So it's done, let's get back to work."* Ben ushers Mark towards the next set of cones. Their backs face the group; we follow slowly. Hamish scuttles past Richard.

Post-training the 'Youth' team are playing a mid-week training match – U19s versus Avonford U19s. I stand with Hamish and Callum as we stay to watch:

HAMISH: *"Fuck me, these are shit,"* (Laughing sadistically)
CALLUM: *"I remember you when you arrived. You couldn't lace these boys' boots"*
HAMISH: *"Give it a rest Cal... I hope we go far in the cup this year, decent TV game. That way everyone will see how shit you are. Better start looking for your touch now lad."*
CALLUM: *"Don't worry about me. You just worry about one of these young'uns taking your place. Keep checking that shoulder for Richard. Don't shit yourself, mate."*
HAMISH: *"What? Only one that needs to worry about losing their place is Char..."*

Both glance towards me, sniggering. I offer a wry smile, but continue watching. Do they really think that? I hate when they get like this. Will joins us after shower, his long dark hair soaking wet swept back from his eyes. Callum continues, *"What do you reckon to Pedro then, Ham?"* A moment of silence. *"That lad trialling? He was shit mate,"* Hamish replied. *"He's better than you,"* Will interrupts. Callum and Will explode with laughter. Hamish smiles but continues to moan, "Fuck off lads... Seriously though, he's been training a couple of times, I thought he played a decent standard or something? He definitely hasn't. Why is Mark letting him train with us? It always breaks down on him. Fuck going in his group; worse than the 23s," more laughter follows. Will turns his head, hair flopped over his eyes from laughing, *"Well fucking hell Ham, just because he plays your position. He did have some good touches, but if you don't like it that much why didn't you say anything earlier?"* A chance unfolds in the game, *"go on son, gotta score,"* Hamish comments. I don't stay to see the finish of the game, *"Cheers lads, catch you later."* I am still in the starting 11. Hamish always gets away with comments like that; I deserve to be in that 11.

Diary Extract, 22nd February: Legs Have Gone

The board goes up. My number in red, Alex stood beneath, his number in green. I drudged to the side of the pitch.

Why won't my legs play well? I know they can. Where is the speed? Where is the endurance? You should endure; are you weak? Listen to Mark, 'read the game early, step in front of the man, be aggressive.' The instructions are clear. I know them.

Substituted again. Mark shakes my hand, he looks me in the eye, "*Well done, son,*" and returns to the corner of the dug-out. The coaches, physio and players on the bench offer high-fives, some water, and obligatory congratulations. I comply. I feel claustrophobic – have I contributed? Did I play well? – My general feeling is 'no.' I watch Alex move with intent: does he read the game? Does he step in front of the man? Does he pass forward? Is he aggressive? Ross, sitting next to the right of me, approved of his every move. Mark spins round to speak to Ben. He catches my eye in the process, they nod and return to watching. I have the feeling they approved of Alex's performance, too. How was I supposed to 'play forward' in the first half – the game is much tighter. Anyone can come on with 20 to play; the clock reads 58 minutes. "*Play forward; play forward*" bouncing around my head. I feel uncomfortable on this bench. My shoulders round, slumped away from the faded wooden bench. My thighs look pale as a peel up the white shorts clinging to my legs; my stomach pressed over the waistband. I have a bellyache; ibuprofen gives me bellyache. My knee aches. Alex gives the ball away – Ha! He isn't better than you – I sip some water - was I good enough to be playing? I'm starting, but I know Mark wasn't happy I missed training last week. He thinks my commitment is wavering. It isn't. I had work. I'm still committed. I wonder if the other players think that; do they think Alex should be playing instead of me?

Even after those times, all those fails, I've always been committed. What will Mark say post-game? If we win, it'll be fine; don't change a winning team. I know what it feels like to be evaluated; to be told 'no.' I think back to all those years ago...

"*Take a seat, Charlie...Thank you for spending the last six weeks with us. We are pleased you were able to train with us and get used to the team, how have you found everything? We keep high standards here. We play the right way; you would have noticed that. Anyway, how old are you again? You are 16, or is it 17?*"

He continues before I can respond... "*We feel you have good technical ability. You don't look out of place with the scholars, but, the thing is, we feel that you are not better than what we have already got... We wouldn't want to insult you with a bad offer so we can't offer you a contract.*"

Silence. Stunned. "*Well, we will keep an eye on your progress. It was good to have met you. Off you go now...Oh, and Charlie, have you put your kit back in the laundry room? Good lad. See you soon; close the door on the way out. Cheers.*"

I drudge back to the dressing room. Academy written on the door. I brush Ryan's leg as I entered to gather my things, *"Any good?"* he asks. *"No, catch you soon lads,"* my voice cracks. My eyes well up; washbag in one hand, boots in the other – 'Not better than what they have already got' – I thought coaches are supposed to make you better? Isn't that the job? Why won't he work with me if he is that good a coach? I glance at Ryan's plump calves, then back to my hands dwarfed by my washbag.

I stare at my right knee; it looks swollen. A stale smell fills the changing room. I glance from my knee to the washbag. Is that the smell? The leather looks faded and worn; it has been everywhere with me. Mark begins the post-game team talk, *"Great performance today. Good result against a very strong side. I'm really happy with the performances across the pitch today. We played with some great energy. Even the old man, Charlie, you got yourself around the pitch today."* The light sound of chuckling fills the room. Mark scans for me, smirking. He continues, *"On to next week now. We will get to work Monday morning. Prepare right; get the kit and let's get out of here."* Music begins to play. I hate that song Hamish plays after every game. The pile of kit always ends up next to me too. *"Fuck sake, I was shit today* [referring to his playing performance]. *I was shit, what do you think?"* I hear Woody announce with an air of pity as he turns towards Alex. I start removing my boots. Woody rocks forward into his hands. Wrestling with his socks, Alex responds, *"You weren't bad mate, don't worry about it. They played high wingers and we didn't have any, so you were left exposed. Keep your chin up. Got the win, didn't we?"* Alex tosses his muddy sock towards the pile.

Later, I sit with Rhys, Hamish and Woody in the corner of the clubhouse, while we deconstruct the details of the game. Staring into his pint of lager, Woody repeats Alex's explanation, *"Don't you think we are exposed by not having wingers. It leaves me so open if they pick up the ball, no one in front of me like."* Hamish nods sipping from his glass, *"Not sure about the formation myself,"* he adds.

Reflective Questions

1   What are the 'seen' and the 'unseen' features within this series of extracts?
2   What role does the 'backstage' between players (and coaches) have in constructing what is 'seen' within the context?
3   How are the tensions between 'performance' (i.e., playing well; 'best 11') and 'compliance' (i.e., fitting-in; 'being committed') manifest throughout the diary extracts?
4   Throughout the diary extracts, how are the boundaries of being 'seen' often taken-for-granted by practitioners?

5   How can the education of practitioners' observations move beyond 'technical' and 'tactical' facets of each sport?

References

Corsby, C. L. T., & Jones, R. L. (2019a). Observation, evaluation and coaching: The local orderliness of 'seeing' performance. *Sport, Education and Society.* https://doi.org/10.1080/13573322.2019.1587399

Corsby, C. L. T., & Jones, R. L. (2019b). Complicity, performance, and the 'doing' of sports coaching: An ethnomethodological study of work. *The Sociological Review.* https://doi.org/10.1177/0038026119897551

Cronin, C., & Armour, K. M. (2015). Lived experience and community sport coaching: A phenomenological investigation, *Sport, Education and Society, 20*(8), 959–975. https://doi.org/10.1080/13573322.2013.858625

Gale, L., Ives, B., Potrac, P., & Nelson, L. (2019). Trust and distrust in community sports work: Tales from the "Shop Floor". *Sociology of Sport Journal, 36*, 244–253. https://doi.org/10.1123/ssj.2018-0156

Jones, R. L. (2006). Dilemmas, maintaining 'face' and paranoia: An average coaching life. *Qualitative Inquiry, 12*(2), 1012–1021. https://doi.org/10.1177/1077800406288614

Jones, R. L. (2009). Coaching as caring (the smiling gallery): Accessing hidden knowledge. *Physical Education and Sport Pedagogy, 14*(4), 377–390. https://doi.org/10.1080/17408980801976551

Jones, R. L., Edwards, C., & Viotto Filho, I. A. T. (2014). Activity theory, complexity and sports coaching: An epistemology for a discipline. *Sport, Education and Society, 21*(2), 200–216. https://doi.org/10.1080/13573322.2014.895713

Lynch, M. (1993). *Scientific practice and ordinary action: Ethnomethodology and social studies of science.* Cambridge/New York: Cambridge University Press.

Potrac P., Jones, R. L., Gilbourne, D., & Nelson, L. (2012). 'Handshakes, BBQs and bullets': Self-interest, shame and regret in football coaching. *Sports Coaching Review, 1*(2), 79–92. https://doi.org/10.1080/21640629.2013.768418

Sparkes, A. (2002). *Telling tales in sport and physical activity: A qualitative journey.* Leeds: Human Kinetics.

Van Maanen, J. (1988). *Tales of the field: On writing ethnography.* Chicago, IL: University of Chicago Press.

7 Filtering and Finding a New Way

A Creative Nonfiction of Soccer Coaches' Professional Learning

Anna Stodter

Introduction

Sport settings are often seen as an arena for athletes' learning, development, and performance, yet those who coach also have their own equally important and impactful professional learning trajectory. This chapter illustrates how sport coaches learn to coach through idiosyncratic combinations of situations and opportunities ranging in formality, addressing a need for a more nuanced evidence base and a learning theory specific to coaching (Cushion & Nelson, 2013). It is based on the published research 'What works in coach learning, how and for whom? A grounded process of soccer coaches' professional learning' (Stodter & Cushion, 2017). This work investigated the learning of 25 youth soccer coaches in the United Kingdom (UK) using a combination of multiple semi-structured interviews, practice-linked video stimulated recall interviews, and formal coach education course observations over the course of one competitive season. The resulting data were used to produce a substantive grounded theory explaining the 'filter process' whereby individuals adopted, adapted, and rejected elements of their learning experiences. Coaches filtered ideas through a 'double-loop' at individual and contextual levels and tried things out through practically-focused cyclical 'reflective conversations.' This process explains how individual coaches learnt different things from apparently similar situations, due to actively filtering ideas to fit in with their individual biography and coaching context. Evidencing and understanding these processes can inform more effective professional development for sport coaches.

The purpose of this story is to extend and authentically communicate a theoretical explanation of how coaches learn, grounded in empirical data. Aspects of the grounded process, presented in story form here, are not intended to present one universal 'truth' of how all coaches learn. While the work captures patterns of coaches' changing knowledge, understanding, and practice that are common enough to extract and present together, as Eraut (2000, p. 133) points out, "tidy maps of knowledge

DOI: 10.4324/9781003038900-10

and learning are usually deceptive." A more nuanced yet accessible way of depicting the findings that acknowledges the idiosyncrasies vital to coaches' individualised learning can be beneficial. Extending the 'scenario' style adopted by Armour (2010) in her chapter on 'the learning coach,' a composite case study was constructed to illustrate these patterns of learning (see also Callary, Werthner, & Trudel, 2012; Cassidy, Jones, & Potrac, 2009). The story aims to encourage readers, particularly those working within sport coaching and the development of coaches, to reflect upon and consider their own biographies and contexts and how these might influence their professional learning. As such, it concludes with five reflective questions that you may wish to consider. Generally, though, it is hoped that readers will be able to find resonance with events they have observed or heard about, recognising similarities and perhaps differences to their own experiences (Smith, 2017).

This research originated from the viewpoint that there is one reality that we can only ever partially approximate and understand (a realist ontology), and that there are multiple interpretations of that reality (an interpretivist epistemology). Representing post-positivist-informed, substantive grounded theory (Strauss & Corbin, 1998) research findings as creative nonfiction (cf. Kendellen & Camire, 2020) sparked worthwhile considerations about the philosophical coherence and compatibility of these different approaches. Hopefully by reflexively attending to epistemology, theory, and methodology (Smith, McGannon, & Williams, 2016), here readers will be allowed to draw their own informed conclusions.

For this creative nonfiction I, the researcher, am positioned as a storyteller, recasting the results of my analysis to produce a story. The central aspects of the grounded process therefore acted as a guide for the content and particular issues I chose to address in the tale. While the story was written by me as an interpretation and representation of the learning process based on research evidence, every piece of writing can be seen as a construction of the author (Ely, Vinz, Anzul, & Downing, 1997). Similarly to how I constructed the original grounded theory, I drew upon my own background in coaching (soccer and rugby union) and having undertaken formal and informal coach education, which no doubt framed my experiences of conducting the research within soccer clubs and at the courses. The scenes are chronologically ordered, highlighting particular findings that summarise the analytic theme of how coaches' learning happens. I developed this narrative based on observational and practice-linked video stimulated recall interview data (see also Stodter & Cushion, 2019) collected in youth soccer coaching and formal coach education settings. Each scenario therefore includes direct and adapted quotations from the participants and excerpts from observational field notes. Sport coaching, and coaches' learning, takes place in contexts influenced by multiple interacting social, political, historical, cultural, and gendered forces (Lewis, Roberts, Andrews, &

Sawiuk, 2020). It is worth noting therefore that I chose to represent the main character as a man in his mid-20s, guided by the typical gender and age characteristics of the participant sample, the data that I drew upon, and the makeup of the qualified coaching workforce in the UK (UK Coaching, 2019). The result is a constructed representation of the process of coaches' learning.

A Season at Vale FC: Filtering and Finding a New Way

The Course

Freddie watches another pristine grey tracksuit-clad football coach enter the meeting room, scanning the setup of six hexagonal tables for allies and a prime position. He sees the spark of recognition and customary jovial yet firm handshakes ensue, accompanied by a solid pat above the elbow – *they must already know each other.* Yet the various club badges in pride of place on tracksuits and kitbags confirms that all the 'candidates' in the room, from grassroots to academy settings, have travelled from all around the country to be here. At another of the tables, a couple of other coaches to-and-fro with stilted small-talk from their seats, reminding Freddie of his first few days at uni a few years ago. Back then, just like last night, he had followed the same ritual: seek out his most recently washed t-shirt and training bottoms (with the Vale FC badge showing alongside his freshly printed initials 'FL'), fold them up in a pile ready to pull on, save time before the early morning three-hour drive.

I look the part, like I belong here, he had thought as he caught sight of his reflection approaching the building's lofty glass-fronted reception area. *Remember to contribute, make the most of the opportunity, but keep your head down – don't put yourself out there as a target, especially right from day one.*

A familiar deep red Vale FC training top catches Freddie's attention and he clocks Steve, his club colleague and coach of the under-15s, brusquely enter and take a seat near the door. Their eyes align briefly with a nod, across the piles of flipchart paper and glossy candidate portfolios adorned with sunny action shots of children playing football. Freddie feels some relief as he thinks, *At least I kind of know someone here so I look connected, and like I'm a decent enough coach to be part of this.*

As the minute hand on the clock above the projector screen approaches vertical, the seat next to Freddie is dragged back and a young woman drops swiftly into it. Hurriedly tucking in at the table, she glances up and around the unfamiliar gazes of the group.

"Morning," she says.

"Hi, I'm Freddie."

"Jill." she replies. "Just in time, eh! What's that you've got there?" she nods at Freddie's portfolio, and the laminated card resting on it.

"Ah yeah, an 'arrival activity,' it says." Freddie explains, picking it up to wave in Jill's direction. "We have to write on the post-it notes some stuff about what we want to get from the course."

Jill half-smiles with amusement and rises awkwardly to reach for the pile of pale-yellow sticky squares at the centre of the table. Before they can do the customary rounds with the rest of the group, the tutor moves out smoothly from behind his laptop set up with PowerPoint slides at the front of the room, hushing the buzz of conversation with a sharp whistle through his teeth.

"Welcome gentlemen...oh, and lady!" he announces, spotting Jill. "As it says up there, I'm Paul Mills – or Millsy if you like, the lead tutor for this first weekend of learning. As you'll know, this is the start of two intense periods, framing a month back at your clubs. It's designed to challenge you, make you think a little, and have a go at some of the latest ideas in developing young footballers."

As Paul continues his introduction, reading out the 'learning outcome' slides, Freddie scribbles down some hopes and expectations with a branded pen. *Check and challenge to make sure I'm doing the right things for my players. Prove my worth as a coach. A boost.*

The Practical

"Right then fellas." Paul barks to the collection of coaches now dispersed alongside the neat grass football pitch, his tone cutting across the warm, blustery afternoon air. "As we introduced back in the classroom, this session is going to showcase how we might apply those principles, with a focus on hitting the highest man fastest. We'll be looking at transition of possession and zipping those passes up to our centre forward or our wingers and playing from there." He sweeps his hand from left to right, thumb and index finger pressed together, indicating the smooth, speedy movements required. Then gesturing to the small magnetic whiteboard propped against his shin, showing a diagram of the pitch with counters set out in team formation, he continues. "I'll be using a realistic game-based practice and chucking in some challenges and supporting questions to recreate those learning situations. So, to start with I need seven in the red bibs, and another seven in blue here. Oh, look at this, Jill's stepping up in midfield, that's what we like to see!"

All eyes promptly shift towards Jill, who now wears a forced smile with the man-sized bib billowing and flapping around her body at each gust of wind.

"Reds shooting this way, blues defending here." Paul continues, pointing to either side of the pitch. "Normal rules, just the same as any match with offsides from halfway."

The 14 volunteers jog at pace into the playing area, some flicking their heels up, side-skipping, assorted dynamic stretches easing long-dormant muscles and joints into action. For the next couple of minutes, the on-looking candidates shuffle in small groups, finding a good vantage point on the small grassy wall alongside the pitch, while silently judging the rusty skills on show.

"Blues, who's your 'keeper?" Paul shouts as he prepares to roll a shiny Umbro football along the grass to begin the game. "Yes Gary, let's play out from you then..."

Seamlessly moving through the linked 'bite size' phases of his session, Paul shapes his tongue against the roof of his mouth and emits a precise, looping whistle across the playing area. "Alright, bring it in then."

As the playing volunteers huff and puff their way towards Paul, the remaining candidates join up in one large group for his debrief. Freddie is one of the first to arrive, his mind as busy as the page of notes and diagrams he's attempted to scrawl down in his pocket-sized notebook while standing on the wall. *Positive interventions. Challenges for individual players. Game realistic. But how to filter through and make sense of all these new ideas?*

"So that was a demonstration right there of how you can do all your coaching *within* the game." Paul declares, then posits, "Can we make all of our practices game related? You might think all your practices are already, but how many of you would use more than two goals in your sessions? How many goals do you have in a game of football?" he scans the group, pausing for effect.

One or two people shuffle uncomfortably, no one willing to answer for fear of being publicly caught out.

"Easy question, isn't it?" he responds to his own probe. "*Two*. So, if you've got four goals in your session, it's not game related. Get rid of it."

Scattering off into murmuring fragments of unsettled coaches, the cohort collects the debris of notebooks and water bottles and begin trudging up the gravel path back to the meeting room. Freddie finds Jill crouched by the wall, swapping her well-used football boots for flip-flops.

"How was that then, nice to get a run around?" he asks.

"Yeah, not bad once those old boys started passing it to me." she counters with a wry smile.

"Fair play. Some of those ideas though, that came across in Millsy's coaching points, they really chime with what I've always thought are the big issues within youth football."

"Yeah? What's that then?" Jill bundles up her boots and plods uphill with Freddie in tow.

"Well, we did a full debate assignment about it in my final year coaching class at uni. Why don't we have any decent young English players coming through? They really need to be playing the game more, like the kids used to in the streets, that's why. Work things out for themselves, make mistakes, let the game be the teacher."

Jill mulls over the debrief as they catch up with Steve, trailing the rest of the group, shoulders characteristically hunched under the bag of footballs he offered to carry back in.

Freddie continues, nodding towards Steve to include him in the musings. "To be honest, I'm keen to try out something like that 'showcase' session back with the lads at Vale – I can really see it going down a storm and working with them."

"You know when he said it's got to be realistic to the game though," Jill reasons. "I get that, and you know I'm fine with that but it's like those extra side goals, that practice works for me and my players – whenever I've done that, it gets them opening their body up, dragging the ball back playing out and then switch the play from one flank to the other, you know?"

"I see what you're saying." Steve contributes with a full-body shrug and a sharp inhalation, eyes focused ahead with his task of lugging the kit inside. "But you know, to pass these modules and assessments you have to do it their way, your freedom has to go out of the window, but it's just for this course. Then you take what you want, the stuff that fits, take that back to your club, use the bits you want there, yeah?"

Vale FC, the U13s

Freddie crouches down, framing the whiteboard with his squat. The players are sprawled around in a crescent-shaped gathering around him, some standing hands on hips, others resting on the damp artificial turf, propped up with their hands behind their backs. Steam rises gently from their heads, visible in the floodlit October evening. Blushed cheeks and passive early-teenage expressions are accompanied by films of sweat forming on foreheads, generated by the warm-up 'stick-in-the-mud' game they've just finished. At this relatively early stage of the season, Freddie is still getting to know the boys, the setup at Vale, everything.

"Okay lads." Freddie begins, scanning his eyes around theirs. Beyond, through the steam-created haze, he registers Steve shouting his players into a managerial huddle on his half of the training pitch.

"To get you started tonight, we'll be doing a quick exercise looking at passing, and the different types of passes we can use. Then we'll be putting that into a game focused on this block's topic, switching play. So, anyone gets me started with some ideas of what kinds of passes we might look to use in a game?" he glances down at the A3-sized whiteboard and grabs the lid from the marker pen, poised to scribe. Then, scanning the generally blank expressions mixed with bemused intrigue, to Freddie's relief, a recently broken voice pipes up with a suggestion.

"Driven."

Now buoyed with more confidence to speak, ideas begin to be shared aloud.

"Floated, like, just clip it."

"Zipped along the ground."

Freddie probes, "Okay, long or short?"

"Umm, could be either." the player shrugs.

"Yes." Freddie jots 'long/short' on the whiteboard as best he can at pace, conscious not to disrupt the momentum of player input.

"A lofted pass."

"Yep, brilliant, any more for anymore?"

A pause hangs above the group like the steam still rising from their heads. "A diagonal cross?"

"Yes, I like your thinking, we're starting to think about the areas of the pitch too now. I think that's plenty to go with, so now find yourself a partner, and go show me. You've got the whole area, just go and express yourselves, give them a go, what can you do? Show me."

Freddie stands up tall, pleased with the short explanation time – *must be less than two minutes. Keep them moving, keep them thinking, exploring.* He's eager with anticipation to see what his players come up with.

Before long, there are footballs flying in multiple directions, boys trotting around within the white-lined space, heads popping up to locate their mate, slender still-growing limbs seeking to strike and control skidding balls. There's no pattern or rhythm as he takes a central line of travel through the area, aware of potential head-height football-missiles in the disorienting 360-degree disarray. He's simultaneously conscious, in his peripheral vision, of a handful of players' parents behind the 10-foot-high fence that borders the pitch, quietly peering through the criss-crossed wire, cold hands stuffed into jeans or coat pockets. He imagines the murmurs between the Dads as they silently compare their sons' abilities, eyebrows raised at the chaotic passing practice.

"What's this guy all about, does he even know what he's doing?"

"Not like any football training in my day."

"They're just running around all over the place – he needs to get them better at fronting up, defending with a bit of passion, closing out these tight games like United, you know."

As he observes a wayward driven pass skid towards the boundary fence, Freddie senses the parents' attention shift towards the open gate by the half-way line.

"That's okay Carlo, what could you do differently? Have another go?" he questions, as he turns to see Don emerge from the clubhouse. *I swear the last time I saw Don he was half that size, and still he was always a man of substantial proportions.*

Don's got his big quilted academy manager's coat on to guard against the autumn chill. It's visibly taut across the midriff he had developed since retiring from playing professionally for Vale in the 90s while simultaneously adding another dimension to his broad, stalwart centre-back defender's shoulders. Don strolls statesman-like through the gate and along the half-way line, taking in the sessions on either side. Reaching the centre circle, he subtly lifts his chin towards Freddie, indicating for him to come over to join him. *He wants a word.*

"Jayden, get your head over that ball." Don instructs one of the players as Freddie picks the quickest route towards him through the untidy tangle of teenage boys and footballs.

"Alright, boss?" Freddie approaches with a nod and a chipper tone. But Don doesn't reply, silently frowning across his empire enclosed within the artificial pitch, salt-and-pepper stubbled jaw clamped shut.

"You doing a game with the lads after this?" he asks, eyes still trained on Jayden's movements, inspecting for the required improvements.

"Yes, I've got a whole-part-whole after this, exploring how we switch the play."

Don nods. "No need for the second bit then, I'll take the lads after your first game and join 'em up with Steve and his lot over there. They need a proper blow out after Saturday and this session ain't it. You can take the injured group and go through what went wrong on the weekend for their feedback portfolios, club room's free if you want it. Probably be about half past, that alright?"

Head falling to glance down at his watch timer, Freddie nods almost imperceptibly at the rhetorical question. "Sure, I'll have them ready for you then." he responds in a low voice, directed more towards the steadily counting digital display on his wrist than to Don.

Freddie's legs feel like they're rooting him to the spot, now weighed down with Don's judgement. *This new way isn't Don's way of doing things, and he's just made it clear who's in charge here by taking the boys off me for drills and sprints.* Feeling almost comically like a new-born elephant, Freddie is unbalanced by the unplanned changes and galumphs around his thoughts to conceive of the resulting adaptations. *This wasn't the way I wanted to try out all my new ideas on challenges from the course…now I'll have to cram them all in to the first game without testing for players' understanding in the later 'whole.'* His session, which previously felt inventive and constructive, now looks muddled and broken. *Now the players are losing interest, taking the piss with ridiculous attempts at trick techniques. This wouldn't have happened if I'd just stuck the club curriculum*, Freddie thinks, as Don continues his appraising lap, turning his gaze to Steve's well-drilled group of under-15s on the other half of the pitch. They're like a bunch of moving display dummies for that recognisable, logical formula of building from the warm-up into rote-learned technical drills, a well-oiled skills practice then precise conditioned game to finish.

Better try and salvage this and get the players into a game pronto – Freddie rummages in his tracksuit pocket to grab a seldom-used whistle, using it to summon them in towards him. As his group assemble, he thinks, *At least I can still try out a couple of the individual challenges I've planned, see if the boys apply any of these passing techniques to the game*

situation. It's all I can do now Don's bound to hang around watching my
every move for the rest of the session.

The Drive Home

"You've just got to let Don be Don," Steve reassures Freddie, pulling his
delivery van out of the club car park on the way home, "remember he's a
product of the club since the glory days and all this new-fangled stuff isn't
really his bag. Too much, too soon."

Freddie slumps down in the passenger seat, willing the regular Tuesday lift to run past his flat as soon as possible. He reflects with a sigh,
"I dunno, I had all those new things I wanted to practice for the course
assessment, all stuff that really made sense to me, and now I just feel a
bit flat from that tonight." Both hands open on his lap, like an old set of
scales, he deliberates, "I'm kinda caught now between, do I keep trying
to do it that way, or do it the old way? I'm coming away thinking, well you
know, what exactly are they all looking for?"

Steve shrugs his already quite hunched shoulders, shuffling to an al-
tered driving position as Freddie slips his phone out of the club branded
rucksack at his feet. Brooding, he catches up on what he's missed over
the last two hours of coaching. Skipping over the various notifications on
the player analysis app – he'll look at those later – there's a text message
from Jill. They'd stayed in touch after the first weekend of the course as
she's coaching the girls' development centre not too far away, in the same
county. They were swapping notes and session plans from the course and
Freddie told her earlier that he planned to do his practice session for the
assessment tonight.

"How was your session?" She had texted.

"Bombed." Freddie wrote back. "Boss took over in front of all the parents, nightmare!"

Jill must have been waiting on the other end of the phone as the ellip-
sis symbols come up right away to show she's typing her response. "Ah,
sorry mate. I'm struggling with it too, they just leave you to get on with it
& no follow up. Tbh I'm just sticking to what I know at this point."

Freddie ponders this, sitting up to peer out at the blur of passing head-
lights and their mirror images on the wet road ahead. He reads it back
to Steve. "What do you think? Seems a bit closed-minded to me. What's
the point in going on the course if you're not open to different ideas? I
guess she hasn't got anyone else there to help her out. I wonder if I can
just adapt some bits to fit in with Don's preferences, you know, not go
too crazy."

"Yeah, well it probably doesn't hurt just to get the qualification done,
tick that box. But that's not a bad shout, to tweak a few little things."
Steve says, concentrating on dodging parked cars along the too-narrow,
former mining town streets. "Personally, it's reinforced a lot of the good

things I already do, and I've just added the bits about the focus on the individual player, I quite liked that. Fits quite well with how I've seen my two daughters growing up, developing in those ways that are different from each other. They each needed different things, you know? Anyway, we've got our club curriculum and you've got all the stuff you've done before, so you've just got to find that balance of what works for you and for your lads. Evolve. And try not to piss Don off too much as you won't have a job by the end of the season!"

***

[*Six months later*]

Vale FC, the U11s

"Okay, good work boys. Last thing now, over to Freddie for a game." Steve directs the Under 11s, who have just completed a skill session on first-touch finishing under his instruction.

Now co-coaches of this younger age group, the two men have settled into a co-operative rhythm, a silently agreed way of working together that somehow balances their often contrasting approaches. The players jog light-footed towards Freddie, their shadows long in the April evening sunlight. A handful of them laugh with each other over a surprise 'nut-meg' trick they'd managed to catch Steve out with during the practice.

"He'd never have let you get away with that at the start of the season, it's just 'cos we've only got one more session left now!"

"Nah, both of 'em are just in a good mood 'cos we're on shooting and finishing tonight, everyone knows that's a fun one."

"He won't be putting you up front for the last game of the season now you made him look daft!"

"Take a quick drink, boys, 30 seconds." Freddie instructs as they reach him, calm and authoritative. "While you're over there, give yourself a personal rating out of 10 on your finishing so far. No need to share it, but we'll be looking to see you improve that rating in the game so think about how you might do that based on Steve's part you've just done. Off you go."

As the players trot in scattered groups over to the sideline in search of their personally labelled water bottles, Freddie chats to Steve, synchronously stretching down every so often to reach the cones, clearing the playing area for the game.

"Almost there, Steve, one more session to go, eh." He says, returning upright to full stature.

"Yeah mate, I'm ready for the season to end now. Then we go all over again, probably with a new set of lads and coaching team again!" Steve replies with a sagacious smile, reminiscent of the hardiest of season-ticket holders debating the annual comings and goings in the Vale supporter's bar.

"And here was me just getting settled in with you!" Freddie quips as the players begin to gather, eyes up awaiting his instructions. "Alright, just while Steve hands out the bibs, remind yourself about how you're going to increase that rating you gave your own finishing. Now, nothing too complicated here, just a small sided game and then once we get going I'll be dipping in and out, setting you some challenges, asking some questions, and we'll see how we go. Wide pitch, nice and short to let you get those shots off, let's set up and get ourselves going from a reds kick-off."

Steve leaves them to it as Freddie scans the unfolding game in front of him, observing team shapes and combinations, mentally noting the key points for particular individuals. *Watch out for Mo pulling that turn he does on his left foot. Ah, there's a frustrated Liam smashing the ball wildly towards the goal again.* Earlier in the season he'd have stepped in already to ask a load of questions, maybe forcing it a bit, maybe unintentionally de-railing the session. But now he's got to know the lads, how they play, and the environment at Vale. *Maybe I haven't learned much new, just those experiences of the stuff from the course last summer basically going wrong, or more accurately not quite right, it's allowed me to re-evaluate and tweak little things each time. It's easier to experiment now Don's paired me off with Steve, and he's not breathing down my neck!* He manages to take Liam aside on his way to fetch another missed shot, the ball fizzing past the crossbar and over the boundary fence.

"Do you need to smash it like that each time?" Freddie prompts, without pressing for an answer.

Liam gives an acquiescent nod, "Yeah, no, I know," as he lopes off to retrieve the ball.

"Liam's like my twin brother, he is," says Steve, joining Freddie behind the goal, "sulks a bit if you get on his back, doesn't like being wrong, certainly not in front of the others."

"Yeah, his understanding is already there, so just a probing question for him." Freddie responds while contemplating his next intervention.

I'll set both teams a challenge to 'try to play off one touch to set up attacks' – though I know they're not actually going to be able to do it every time and I wouldn't want them to do that either. The challenge gives each player the opportunity to make decisions themselves, based on what I've already said earlier in the session.

After Freddie sets the challenge and lets the players try it out for a few minutes, Steve jumps in with some supporting questions to try and draw out the coaching points from his earlier skills practice. Five minutes on, though, Mo's still doing that multi-touch turn in loads of space on the left. Freddie reasons, *it's slowing down his team's attack every time, so I'll pull him aside.*

"Mo, remember the challenge I set – next time that happens, move yourself early so you're already turned to play with just one touch on the ball. It's much quicker so it means you can get that ball up to the forwards in lots more space."

"Okay, I'll try that."

Sure enough, by the closing stages of the session, Freddie's done enough to step back and enjoy a satisfied assessment of the outcomes with Steve. They stand in a slowly shrinking final patch of sunlight near the fence, hands clasped behind backs.

"Liam's looking like he's getting into some nifty little areas now, he clearly gets it." says Steve.

"Yeah, he's a good lad when he just keeps it calm." Freddie replies. "I'm still trying to decide whether the more game-based coaching works as well for him right now as it does for a few of the others. There's a few things I'd still like to explore further and try out there. With this approach though, that whole attacking shape should work well on Saturday, if they bring it on the day they'll have come on a load even just in the past three weeks. And I'll get you a beer to celebrate!"

"Makes a change, you getting a round in, I'll hold you to that." Steve smiles back, as Mo sets up a slick final pass into the penalty area, connecting with a well-timed centre-forward run tipping the ball smartly into the bottom corner of the goal. Freddie blows an over-exaggerated final whistle for effect – *that's good, for now.*

Reflective Questions

1   Freddie, Steve, and Jill all attend the same formal learning situation (the course), but they each learn different things. Why?
2   Consider your own biography – the network of past experiences, knowledge, beliefs, and dispositions you bring to every learning situation. How does this influence your reading and interpretation of the story?
3   How do different aspects of the story resonate with your own experiences of learning within your profession?
4   Based on your reading of the story, try to come up with a set of principles important for coaches' learning. Now compare these with the grounded process in the original paper (Stodter & Cushion, 2017) – what are the similarities or differences?
5   How could the coach education course be designed differently to more effectively impact on the coaches' learning?

References

Armour, K. M. (2010). The learning coach…the learning approach: professional development for sports coach professionals. In C. Cushion & J. Lyle (Eds.), *Sports coaching: Professionalisation and practice* (pp. 153–164). Edimburgh: Churchill Livingstone.

Callary, B., Werthner, P., & Trudel, P. (2012). How meaningful episodic experiences influence the process of becoming an experienced coach. *Qualitative Research in Sport, Exercise and Health, 4*(3), 420–438. https://doi.org/10.1080/2159676X.2012.712985

Cassidy, T., Jones, R., & Potrac, P. (2009). *Understanding sports coaching: The social, cultural, and pedagogical foundations of coaching practice* (2nd ed.). Abingdon: Routledge.

Cushion, C., & Nelson, L. (2013). Coach education and learning: Developing the field. In P. Potrac, W. Gilbert, & J. Denison (Eds.), *Routledge handbook of sports coaching* (pp. 359–374). Abingdon: Routledge.

Ely, M., Vinz, R., Anzul, M., & Downing, M. (1997). *On writing qualitative research: Living by words.* London: Falmer.

Eraut, M. (2000). Non-formal learning and tacit knowledge in professional work. *British Journal of Educational Psychology, 70*, 113–136. doi:10.1348/000709900158001.

Kendellen, K., & Camiré, M. (2020). A creative non-fiction story of an athlete's journey through the life skills application process. *Qualitative Research in Sport, Exercise and Health.* https://doi.org/10.1080/2159676X.2020.1803392

Lewis, C. J., Roberts, S. J., Andrews, H., & Sawiuk, R. (2020). A creative writing case study of gender-based violence in coach education: Stacey's story. *Women in Sport and Physical Activity Journal, 28*, 72–80. https://doi.org/10.1123/wspaj.2018-0046

Smith, B. (2017). Generalizability in qualitative research: Misunderstandings, opportunities and recommendations for the sport and exercise sciences. *Qualitative Research in Sport, Exercise and Health, 10*(1), 137–149. https://doi.org/10.1080/2159676X.2017.1393221

Smith, B., McGannon, K. R., & Williams, T. L. (2016). Ethnographic creative nonfiction. In G. Molnár & L. Purdy (Eds.), *Ethnographies in sport and exercise research* (pp. 49–73). Abingdon: Routledge.

Stodter, A., & Cushion, C. J. (2017). What works in coach learning. How, and for whom? A grounded process of soccer coaches' professional learning. *Qualitative Research in Sport, Exercise and Health, 9*(3), 321–338. https://doi.org/10.1080/2159676X.2017.1283358

Stodter, A., & Cushion, C. J. (2019). Evidencing the impact of coaches' learning: Changes in coaching knowledge and practice over time. *Journal of Sports Sciences, 37*(18), 2086–2093. https://doi.org/10.1080/02640414.2019.1621045

Strauss, A., & Corbin, J. (1998). *Basic of qualitative research: Techniques and procedure for developing grounded theory* (2nd ed.). Thousand Oaks, CA: Sage.

UK Coaching. (2019). *Coaching in the UK, 2019 Coach Survey.* Online resource retrieved July 31, 2020, from https://www.ukcoaching.org/getattachment/Resources/Topics/Research/Coaching-in-The-UK/CPS_Coaches-_FINAL.pdf?lang=en-GB

8 The Emergence and Perpetuation of a Destructive Culture in a British Olympic Sport

Niels Boysen Feddersen

Introduction

The recent surge in disclosures from athletes who have experienced bullying or abuse in sport indicates that destructive or even toxic cultures are very much a part of the sporting arena. Some might dismiss these cases as extreme; and yet, as numbers grow, it becomes clear why the sports sector is under more scrutiny than ever before (Grey-Thompson, 2017). The news and statements from athletes provide us with insights into their individual experiences. However, there are few accounts that consider the systemic features beyond a single offender. Building upon this, the current chapter provides a unique lens into the experience of being in a culture, which went through a phase with destructive features. The current chapter might help to vicariously prepare researchers who might dive into researching destructive cultures (see Feddersen, Morris, Littlewood, & Richardson, 2020).

The current chapter is based on an 18-month longitudinal study into power relations and organisational culture change. From this study, we published a paper examining how destructive cultures emerge and perpetuate in British elite sport (Feddersen, Morris, Littlewood, et al., 2020), which is also the basis for the creative nonfiction below. The second study (Feddersen, Morris, Abrahamsen, Littlewood, & Richardson, 2020) examined how societal changes and systemic power relations between organisations such as UK Sport and Sport England influence culture change in national governing bodies (NGB). And finally, the third study (Feddersen, Morris, Storm, Littlewood, & Richardson, 2020) examined the power relations between individuals and groups to show how power determined the culture change direction taken by an NGB. The three studies are interwoven and provide important context for the fluid nature and violence of some cultural shifts. Yet, as mentioned, the current chapter takes its point of departure from the first study.

The study that forms the basis for the creative nonfiction (cf. Feddersen, Morris, Littlewood, et al., 2020) found that a destructive culture emerged in an NGB during a time of radical changes. Here, some individuals felt that their livelihoods were threatened by a group of outsiders

DOI: 10.4324/9781003038900-11

now running the talent pathway (e.g., the talent manager and coach education manager). Individuals who had been with the particular sport for a long time felt that the outsiders were only with the sport as a stepping-stone to the next job. Some individuals and groups entered into conflict with the NGB to preserve their way of doing things. Over time, the conflict grew in severity, and antagonistic behaviours led to the emergence of a destructive culture. As the conflict escalated, individuals at all levels of/within the NGB rationalised their destructive actions by denying responsibility (e.g., failing to provide oversight) and using the malleability of language (e.g., shifting the meaning of words) to make behaviours seem less severe. People who spoke out against destructive behaviours felt pursued by others who questioned their competencies and legitimacy to further delegitimise their concerns. It is critical to mention that the NGB recognised the destructive features of their culture and have since gone to great lengths to change for the better. They are currently the recipient of funding from Sport England and UK Sport because of their work on promoting inclusion and psychological safety in the talent pathway.

Organisational culture is a contentious discussion as an academic field. The most popular approach to researching organisational cultures is by viewing a group or organisation through a lens of shared values, assumptions, beliefs, and artefacts. Around 70% of sports psychology research uses this framework (see Wagstaff & Burton-Wylie, 2018). However, Joanne Martin, a key figure in organisational culture research, argues that the view is: 'a seductive promise of harmony and value homogeneity that is empirically unmerited and unlikely to be fulfilled' (Martin, 2004, p. 7). So, if culture is not a set of shared values, then what? The current chapter and the three papers mentioned above treat culture as differentiated, meaning that there are many subunits (e.g., groups and individuals) who have different values and beliefs (Meyerson & Martin, 1987). Instead of examining what is shared, the three studies examine how subunits meet, collide, or conflict. Given recent events (e.g., allegations of bullying in British Gymnastics, the Nassar abuse scandal, the Essendon doping scandal, or bullying in Danish swimming), it seems incongruous to assume that all individuals in these organisations share the same values. Equally, it is an easy answer to point the finger at one culprit. Instead, looking beyond values and assumptions to understand how power relations influence how subunits meet, allows researchers to draw closer a picture of how conflict might lead to a destructive culture.

Creative nonfiction is, for me, a way of showing you what it was like being in a transient destructive culture as-it-happened. It is also a way to let you peek into the turmoil by connecting with you through a language that stirs up emotions. Consider Robin Williams' line from the film Good Will Hunting (1997):

> If I asked you about art, you'd probably give me the skinny on every art book ever written. Michelangelo, you know a lot about him. Life's

work, political aspirations, him and the pope, sexual orientations, the whole works, right? But I'll bet you can't tell me what it smells like in the Sistine Chapel. You've never actually stood there and looked up at that beautiful ceiling; seen that.

The question Robin Williams asks is whether you can know something without having been there. For the purpose of the current chapter, then, can you actually know what it feels like being in a destructive culture? Being there, feeling the intense pressure of conflict and colliding agendas? Creative nonfiction provides a lens, which brings you up close with lived experiences. That is what creative nonfiction as a form of scientific communication can bring to readers.

The NGB in the current study is anonymised to protect those involved with the study. All names and places are replaced[1] to secure their continued anonymity.

Being in a Destructive Culture in Elite Sports: A Creative Nonfiction

June 2017: Preconditions or Where We Were

The bell above the door chimes as it is pushed open. Atticus peers into the long room looking for someone he has never met. Outside the cars a whirring past in the late afternoon summer sun. Inside, he finds who he is looking for.

'One cappuccino, please.' 'Over here,' he gestures to the barista.

Atticus is the Talent Manager and the head of the new Talent Pathway. He is young. And found himself in the organisation on maternity cover before taking over the talent programme on another maternity cover.

He sits down, and continues:

'Thank you for getting in touch. Your proposal sounded interesting, and we are just starting a new talent development programme, so we could definitely use a pair of critical eyes on our work.

So, basically, we lost a lot of funding after last year's games and had to let a lot of people go. We really regressed to a kitchen table setup. All the elite and talent stuff went into the hands of volunteers.

And now we are coming in. Me, the talent manager, but I am coming from a background in track and field, and so is the new admin. The coach developer guy is a rugby man. A lot of people are definitely looking at us going "you have no idea about what is going on here".'

Atticus sips his cappuccino as he is looking across the table. For answers. For some kind of feedback.

'So, that is where we are. We have two years of funding. But really only until December '18 because we have to submit our report to Sport England on how we have met the performance targets. And we are already behind. Our first camp is in August and we are just trying to move fast.'

August 2017: A Challenge to Survival or Social Position

'Maybe we could try a whole-part-whole approach instead.'

Marvin is obviously not happy with what happened today. He is sitting, almost lying down in his chair in an office in a gym in London. At least it is designated as an office. But it is four white and paper-thin walls and a low, brooding ceiling. It is closer to a cardboard box in a gym. Atticus shifts his gaze from Marvin to Niccolò. Trouble is the head coach usually has the last word. And that word is Niccolò's.

Marvin goes on: 'The athletes were obviously not engaged. Did you see them? And we were just standing around. We are five coaches, and it is only you who's running training. We might as well go home.'

Niccolò is pursing his lips.

Atticus shifts his gaze again. Like that day in the café, he is looking for answers. For some kind of feedback. He draws a breath.

'Marvin is right. It was not what we were hoping for today.'

There is a bit of bitterness in air. Something that almost tastes like over-steeped tea.

'We have five coaches here, included you two. Right? We did that to change the ratio. Fewer athletes per coach. You need to use them, all the coaches. Okay? Niccolò?'

'It is important to have progression' Niccolò shrugs.

There is a clear rhythm to Niccolò. Both in his training and his voice. Something hard to pinpoint. Maybe something from Eastern Europe.

'First. Foot work. Then, drills. Last, full.'

Marvin's face darkens.

'That is what we just did. We lost them before the drills. Change it up. We do this all the time in our club. First we do the full thing, then back to drills or footwork to practice parts of it, then back to full. You must see it!'

Another pursing from Niccolò and a shrug, 'Okay, we'll try it.'

The Next Morning

'I don't even know what I am doing here.'

Marvin the thundercloud is pacing back and forth.

'You were in the room yesterday. You heard that we agreed to doing something else. Might as well f*** off home now. All he cares about is his way. We all came in with the new schedule, you know. Turns out he changed it all last night.'

Marvin scowls at Niccolò.

'Atticus can't do s***. Nobody cares what a track guy thinks about coaching in this sport. He might be the manager. But he has no power.'

That Afternoon

'Oh. You are still here?'

The rhythm of Niccolò's timbre disturbs the quite air. He is the only coach, the only one, left in the gym. Everyone else left after the debrief.

'You see what I have to deal with. After I explain to Atticus how it works in a sports life, that the coach setup the programme. Doesn't matter what coach. Football coach, rugby coach, any coach. I set up the programme and the one who is responsible for the whole thing, like the manager, needs to do everything to make the programme happen.'

October 2017: Further Challenge to Survival or Social Position

'I just came from a meeting with Sport England. We have all these targets that we basically have to live up to. But I don't know if they are fit for the new programme because we basically just inherited them from the old one. So, I am trying to change them. But it's a bit hard.'

Atticus slumps into a lounge chair in the office. The office is in the basement of the training centre. There are no windows, only concrete walls painted in an eerie white hue. His attention is—for a moment—caught by a flicker in the fluorescent lighting.

'Niccolò has to get with the program. If he is causing a drag on the system and doesn't want to change then he is out. Our training is archaic. Thirty athletes on a line learning to walk slowly. Not even in kit. It. Does. Not. Work.'

His eyes glaze over.

'The Sport England guys said that I should think of them as a suit of armour. But I'm left trying to play catch up with the goals that they set for us. And now I have to get rid of people who have been in this sport for decades.'

The energy seeps out of the room as Atticus slumps further into the chair. All that is left now is a staleness.

'You know,' he continues. 'We get all of this feedback from the community. And it is quite aggressive assaults on us. "You just don't know what you're doing. This is rubbish. What's going on?" When we haven't even started. It's hard.'

Static silence inhabits the room for a while.

Looking up, 'what do you think? Get rid of him?'

December 2017: The Emergence of a Destructive Culture

Rhett is coming up the stairs. He is wearing his official kit and shifts his shoulder bag nervously as he nears. Rhett is the administrator of the talent programme. He is probably the most knowledgeable person in the whole organisation, although he rejects that notion.

'Oh, hey,' he says. 'You alright?'

It's early on a Saturday morning the last weekend before Christmas. And here he is. In a steel box of a warehouse turned elite training gym in an industrial area in the outskirts of London.

'Atticus was telling me that you would be here this weekend,' he says. 'Is he here yet? And where is everyone?'

He is scanning the gym for athletes and coaches. Three coaches are lounging on plastic chairs around a small table, planning the training schedule with the lead coach. Three athletes are scattered around the gym. Four coaches and three athletes.

'Is this it? The morning practice is due to start in 15 minutes, and athletes are supposed to arrive half an hour early, right?'

Rhett's face falls into a different shade of winter grey.

'19. 19 were supposed to be here,' he mutters.

Pulling his hair, he shifts the shoulder bag off and dumps it on the floor. His movement is more erratic and disconnected now. Like a glitching robot. Apparently, not only people in movies pull their hair. It happens in real life too. Rhett scuttles into the coaches' office and lets his bag drop onto the desk as he pulls his computer from the main pocket. The few athletes who are here start moving through their warmup rituals. Rhett looks visibly shaken. As if a dreary grey November has taken residence in his soul.

'I confirmed with everyone this week,' Rhett continues. 'I emailed them with the correct times, the timetable, and the instructions from the coaches. Didn't I?'

He pulls up the emails he sent and checks and rechecks if they came back as Message not delivered.

'Yes, 19 signed on for the camp,' he confirms in a shaky voice.

19 athletes are currently the bulk of the U23, the U19, and the U16 national team in this event—the beginning of a new talent pathway. 16 missing.

'I have to call them. The athletes or parents. I need to know why they are not here. I, honestly, have no idea about what is going on.'

Rhett nods and scrambles on the computer to find the contacts of the athletes affiliated with the programme. As he is pulling up contacts, Atticus pops his head into the office.

'You alright?' he says with a big smile. 'The group is looking pretty slim?'

Rhett greys further as he focuses more intensely on moving the cursor to the appropriate icons.

'We had 19 confirmed today, and only three showed up,' Rhett says.

The contrast is glaring. Atticus, beaming as if he was handed the keys to the city and Rhett, who's thick, heavy mood seems to the suck the soul out of good people.

'Oh,' Atticus says. 'That's not good.'

Atticus is still looking cheery as ever, shrugs, and leaves the office.

At the edge of the court, Atticus turns: 'So, I was away at a competition last week alone with 12 athletes, and we were talking. None of them had ever been to the talent camps. So, the talking went into that. Why they hadn't been. They just went "Norman tells us not to go, so we don't bother."'

He seems to be excited over athletes from the youth national team not coming to talent camps because Norman tells them not to.

Rhett looks back in surprise: 'I know Norman. I even had dinner with him and the coaches last time I was down. He picked the spot. Indian food. It was a really great night.'

'Yeah!' Atticus nods with an almost deranged, wide-eyed look that shows everyone knows the implications. 'But then I get back to the office on Monday, and everything comes out. You remember how this one parent effectively donated equipment to the club and expected their child to get selected to the youth national team? Apparently, Norman and the parent kept discussing it. And Norman kept saying they'd get their kid selected. All of this came out.'

'Norman claimed to be able to get the kid on the team?' Rhett asks.

'Yes. We kept having the same argument with that coach and the parent about selection because Norman is one of our selectors. But then this week, the parent's personal assistant mistakenly forwarded us a string of emails. You know if you go down to the bottom of the email you can see the old ones?'

The contrast of what is happening is tangible. Rhett is trying to call parents, making notes, and looking grey as ever. Atticus is looking like he is about to burst with excitement. Atticus leads the way out of the office to give Rhett some time and privacy to work. At the courts, he turns and proceeds:

'Yes, so we could see that Norman had written that he would try to make it happen.'

'Yes! I know,' he says with wide eyes. 'So, my boss, you know Ripley, kicks off because Norman is a personal friend and has been lying all this time. And you know Ripley was away for an international conference at the time, and it just became too much. One day we just get an email that Ripley is not taking emails for the next seven days. Completely stamped out. Eventually, they had to get Norman's boss involved. Norman's boss was obviously defending Norman without knowing the ins and outs of the situation. Now we're at a point where everything is out. Norman knows he did something terrible and is keeping a low profile.'

Atticus continues.

'You know he isn't speaking to me anymore? No, he hasn't spoken to me for months because of this. You remember we had a thing about the bookings too? So, we had booked on for all these camps here at the centre. And Norman is in charge of the booking schedule here. So, in effect, he goes through and just takes days out here and there. Not a full two-day weekend camp. Just, like "You can't have this Sunday. You can't have this day." You know the one over Christmas? He just takes out the day in the middle for no other reason than killing the whole programme.'

'Only four answered the first time I called them.' Just like that, Rhett snaps Atticus back into the present.

Rhett is clutching his notebook with scribbles and names as he goes on: 'So, they just gave a bunch of excuses, like one of the parents said: "the mother is in charge of the emails, and the father is in charge of the phone, and there is no communication." One of the athletes thought his mother had confirmed that he would not be attending, and his mother thought that her son had confirmed that he will not be attending. I also spoke to one who said that the flat had come down with norovirus. Some said they had to see elderly family members. Three are away to one of the regions for a coaching course which had been combined with a talent camp. But not run by us.'

Atticus glares at Rhett as it sinks in.

'Well,' Atticus begins. 'You know I've seen you take care of all of that this week. Those excuses are just ridiculous. It is not on you.'

Rhett nods and retreats to the office to get in contact with the remaining athletes.

Atticus is looking for the words, 'Hmmm, I don't know where that leaves your work. But I am speaking to Ripley on Monday, and I'll give you a call after.'

December 2017: The Perpetuation of a Destructive Culture

Here, in the hallway outside the university gym, the fluorescent lights hum louder. It is an insisting droning sound interspersed with an electric flickering. Each flickering seemingly makes the strip lighting shine brighter. Whiter. It is a creeping, low-level anxiety that making the walls itch.

It has been six months now. Working with a national governing body and researching how to develop a new talent pathway. So far, it never ceases to be interesting. On any given day it has been a maelstrom of hidden agendas and conflicting ambitions. But the past few days accelerated the currents of conflict.

The metallic sound of Atticus' voice comes through the earpiece on my black smartphone with its distinct fruit on the back: 'It has been a mental toll. All the assaults on us. That we don't know what we are doing. I feel that I am trying to do the right thing. But they are constantly trying to catch me out. I attribute most of the fallout to the problems we've had with Norman and that my colleagues have given me absolutely no support. Actually, saying that they would prefer to support Norman because they were the person who is in it for the long run. And you're saying that Ripley called you just now. Wow. That's my fault. They seem worried about who knows what. I said I'd spoken to you. I'm sorry if it led to an uncomfortable conversation. I had a tough one.'

There is a bit of lull. It is quite crinkling in the receiver before Atticus continues. 'Ripley called to make it clear that the whole matter had been looked over by a disciplinary committee. It is clear to everyone that Norman had done something wrong. And it could not be condoned. However, it is clear that it is not their intention to fire or relieve him of his post. At least not for the time being. Basically, we need new selection procedures or policies to replace the old ones that people can game. I mean, donations are commonplace, and they allow us to send twelve athletes rather than nine to international competitions. All because of money donated from the community to clubs. But we cannot just send athletes because their parents buy us a new set of training cones.'

There's the sound of car in the background making Atticus inaudible for a brief moment.

'... as I said basically removing Norman would blow up an event. But where do we draw the line? Who decides? Someone else in the organisation even tried to make me drop it by mentioning how one of my friends, Rosalie, was a bad person. They argued that Rosalie's mother had pushed for their selection for international competitions and for the old world-class programme. They even said that Rosalie's mother had, in fact, pushed so hard that it could have been interpreted as...'

Another car whizzes by in the background.

'They just want to push me by making it very clear that even my friends are not... may not be as pure as they seem to be. So, this is how it happens. One guy leans on another, and everyone else looks away.'

September 2018

The fruit-clad phone hums.

Atticus: Morning. I hope you're having a good weekend.

Atticus: Bad news. Norman won the personality of the year award. Good news. I've handed in my resignation and will be moving on in December.

Reflective Questions

The creative nonfiction aimed to put you, the reader, in the room as a spectator and as close to my own shoes as possible. A vital point is that I experienced the events in one way, and others may have experienced them very differently. As a silent observer, I tried to let you be a witness to the flux in power relations. And the differences in my experiences and what you saw underpin the reflective questions. The prose shows that some critical events can happen very quickly. The acknowledgement that people experience things differently based on their past experiences, socio-economic status, gender, nationality, etc. leads to the following reflective questions:

1   What do you see in the creative nonfiction that I did not?
2   How would you support the organisation moving forward?
3   How do we determine what destructive behaviours are?

As a note, it is incredibly easy being a consequentialist and judging everyone after events have unfolded. However, we spend most of the time stumbling around in the dark, and it is not until a light gets switched on that we gravitate towards it. You can reflect on the questions based on what you have read and what you know is happening in sport. But try to put yourself in the shoes of someone who is navigating it in real-time. It might change how you view things.

Note

1 The real names are replaced with the names of fictional characters: Atticus Finch, Marvin (the Paranoid Android), Niccolò Machiavelli, Rhett Butler, Norman Bates, Ellen Ripley, and Rosalie after a still living tortoise who survived the London Blitz in 1940.

References

Feddersen, N. B., Morris, R., Abrahamsen, F. E., Littlewood, M. A., & Richardson, D. J. (2020). The influence of macrocultural change on national governing bodies in British Olympic sports. *Sport in Society*, 1–17. https://doi.org/10.1080/17430437.2020.1771306

Feddersen, N. B., Morris, R., Littlewood, M. A., & Richardson, D. J. (2020). The emergence and perpetuation of a destructive culture in an elite sport in the United Kingdom. *Sport in Society*, *23*(6), 1004–1022. https://doi.org/10.1080/17430437.2019.1680639

Feddersen, N. B., Morris, R., Storm, L. K., Littlewood, M. A., & Richardson, D. J. (2020). A longitudinal study of power relations in a British Olympic Sport Organization. *Journal of Sport Management*, 1–13. https://doi.org/10.1123/jsm.2020-0119

Grey-Thompson, T. (2017). Duty of care in sport review. *Independent report. UK Government.* https://www. gov.uk/government/publications/duty-of-care-in-sport-review

Martin, J. (2004). Organizational culture: Research paper series. *Culture, 1847.*

Meyerson, D., & Martin, J. (1987). Cultural change: An integration of three different views. *Journal of Management Studies, 24*(6), 623–647.

Wagstaff, C. R. D., & Burton-Wylie, S. (2018). Organisational culture in sport: A conceptual, definitional and methodological review. *Sport & Exercise Psychology Review, 14*(2), 32–52.

9 Re-Building and Re-Discovering after Emotionally Abusive Experiences

Gretchen Kerr and Erin Willson

Introduction

Disclosures of abuse by athletes have heightened public and scholarly attention recently. The high-profile cases of Nassar in USA Gymnastics, and Bennell of U.K. Football, are two of many examples of abuse that have been allowed to perpetuate across years and hundreds of young victims. Although cases of sexual abuse predominate in the media, a growing body of scholarly work in sport sociology, sport psychology, and coaching, has shown that experiences of emotional abuse are the most commonly experienced form of abuse (Alexander et al., 2011; Kerr et al., 2019; Parent & Vaillancourt-Morel, 2020; Vertommen et al., 2016). Emotional abuse has been defined as "a pattern of deliberate non-contact behaviours by a person within a critical relationship role that has the potential to be harmful" (Stirling & Kerr, 2008, p. 178). Although verbal comments that are derogatory, degrading, belittling, or threatening are typically thought of as characterizing emotional abuse, this form of harm may also occur through physical acts such as throwing objects in anger (but not to strike the other person), or through the deliberate denial of attention and support such as when a coach chooses not to coach a team during a training as punishment for a poor performance (Stirling & Kerr, 2008). Not only has emotional abuse been shown to be common, but it tends to be accepted as a typical and even required ingredient for talent development in sport (Stafford et al., 2015; Stirling & Kerr, 2013). Given this acceptance, emotional abuse in sport has been normalized, and thus is often not labelled as abusive or thought of as a contributor to mental health challenges. On the contrary, in the nonsport literature, the effects of emotional abuse on mental health are well-documented. The research on the effects of emotional abuse on athletes' health is in its infancy but suggests that links with depression and anxiety exist (Kerr et al., 2020; Stirling & Kerr, 2013).

In this chapter we focus on experiences of emotional abuse drawing upon data collected and analysed for the paper, "It was the Worst Time

DOI: 10.4324/9781003038900-12

in My Life: The Effects of Emotionally Abusive Coaching on Female Canadian National Team Athletes" published in *Women in Sport and Physical Activity Journal* (Kerr et al., 2020). This study used a constructivist perspective to understand athletes' subjective experiences of emotionally abusive coaching practices and their perspectives of the long-term effects of these experiences. The study involved a single interview with each of eight, elite, retired female athletes from aesthetic sports. Female athletes were chosen because of the higher prevalence rates of emotional abuse reported among female compared with male athletes (Kerr et al., 2019). Elite, retired athletes were the focus given the evidence indicating that experiences of emotional abuse increase with competitive level (Gervis et al., 2016), and reflections about emotionally abusive experiences deepen upon retirement when athletes are out of the sport context (Kerr & Dacyshyn, 2000). Consistent with the findings from the child maltreatment literature, the athletes in this study reported increased fear, anxiety, depression, and suicide ideation. Their social relationships in sport were affected and all of the athletes required professional help post-retirement to deal with their emotionally abusive experiences. According to these athletes, the ways in which they responded to, addressed, and resolved their experiences of emotional abuse in sport changed across time – during their careers, during the retirement transition, and post-retirement transition.

The following creative nonfiction piece is designed to provide the reader with a glimpse into female athletes' experiences of emotionally abusive coaching practices in aesthetic sports. The athletes who engaged in this study had competed in international level competitions such as World Championships and the Olympic Games. For most of their competitive careers and certainly once they reached international levels of competition, they were training six days and approximately 30–35 hours per week. Outside of their training, they also had weight-training, ballet classes, and sessions with a physiotherapist, sport psychology consultant, and nutritionist. The athletes had been retired from their competitive careers for 4.5 years on average.

We chose this paper as our creative nonfiction piece given the powerful emotional engagement and expressions of the athletes in the interview. Writing this piece enabled us to shift from 'what' was said in the interview and published in the article, to the emotions associated with what was said. In essence, we were able to move from the spoken words and 'meaning units' to the embodiment of the athletes' experiences. During the interviews, we were struck by the ways the athletes fought back tears, with tears sometimes breaking through the armour the athletes wore. We chose one athlete to represent the various stories told through the interviews.

A Broken Spirit

Getting Ready for Training

The alarm clock rings with that all too familiar sound and I reflexively think, *oh...no, not yet...please... it can't be time to wake up yet. Another day of training waiting for me.* As I begin to think about the day, I feel a tightness in my stomach, my heart rate increases, and my mouth gets so dry I can barely separate my lips. I think through the plans for the day – having breakfast, driving to practice, having physio after practice... and the more I think, the more my worrying worsens. I lie in bed worrying about how well I will perform, worrying about what kinda mood my coach will be in. I try to prepare mentally for her glaze up and down my body and the look of disapproval on her face if she thinks I look heavy in spite of hardly eating. I wonder how I'll ever get up the energy to get myself out of bed and to training. I just have to hang in there for a few more months, until the [Olympic] Games are over. Then I'll quit. *You can do this* I think as I give myself a final pep talk before moving and getting out of bed. I just keep telling myself, *you just have to get through the day.*

As soon as I move, I feel fire in my low back. My hand runs there, massaging the sore area. It is hot, and so tight.

'Mmmmh... MUM, mummy I need your help please...could you just help me pull my socks up?'

My mum walks in the room, frowning.

'No need to look at me like that, you know how it is, especially in the morning. I just need to get moving to loosen it up.'

Yes. Moving. As if that was easy.

I sit on the bed and stare at my reflection. Shoulders sagging, bags under my eyes, face the colour of milk. I feel no energy this morning. With the [Olympic] Games approaching, the intensity of training is insane, with never enough time for rest and recovery. My back has been aching after training for years but the intensity of training now has made my back pain unbearable.

At Training

When I get to the pool, the smell of the chlorine brings back the knot in my stomach that I started the day with. As I begin to warm-up, I feel the coldness of the coaches' gaze. It feels like they're looking right through me, examining what I ate yesterday by the look of my waist. I'm sure they know how much body fat I have just by looking at me. They sit on the other side of the pool, with stern looks on their faces – never smiling. Their glaze makes me worry – I worry about not being perfect in my appearance or in my skills. I can't seem to stop the flood of negative thoughts ... *What if I miss the lift? What if my alignment is off? What if I'm a split second behind my teammates?* My mind is spinning. A perfect prescription for making an error... focusing on avoiding what not to do instead of what to do. Sure enough, I miss the timing of a skill ruining the coordination with the others. Here it comes... the coach's wrath:

[Coach] "WHAT ARE YOU DOING YOU STUPID GIRL? DO YOU HAVE A BRAIN?"

[Silence]

I whisper *"I'm sorry"* to my teammates knowing that everyone will be punished for my error. These are the rules of engagement... coach commands and controls and we, as athletes, have no voice and do as we're told.

[Coach] "AGAIN," a roaring voice from the pool deck directs us to repeat the sequence.

Silently, we do as we're told and repeat the sequence. This time, a teammate makes an error, and we have to stop. I hear the anticipated whispered *"sorry"* from her and I quickly give her a reassuring glance knowing what's coming.

[Coach] "We have too many girls for the team – looks like you two want to be the alternates," referring to my teammate and I who made the errors.

The pool water gives my tears a welcomed disguise.

I leave the pool after practice feeling small and insignificant – I wish I was invisible. Having to sit still in the car on the drive home just provided another long opportunity to re-live the eight hours of being put down by my coach. Negative thoughts flood my mind, *I am not good enough; I am not pretty enough; I am not thin enough; I am definitely going to lose my spot on the team.* Throwing my bag on the floor once I arrive home, I hardly say a word to my mum who is waiting with a snack, which I refuse. As she greets me, I see her upward turned corners of her lips drop as she notices my red, swollen eyes. She can tell how my practice was but asks anyway – as she always does. "Fine," I mumble before going to my room and shutting my door for the rest of the night, feeling the anxiety of tomorrow's practice already washing over me and the warmth of tears against my cheeks.

Just an Empty Shell

I made the team, and the Olympics are over. For all of those tough years leading up to the Games I had a picture in my mind of what retirement post-Olympics would be like. This picture included a wonderful sense of pride in reaching my goal of performing on the world stage at the Olympic Games. It also included tremendous relief in not having to fight through physical pain every day and escaping from the continuous stream of negative comments from my coaches. Imagine being able to wake up and not have a pit in my stomach knowing what the day's training would involve. This picture revealed a new me, not having to worry about the number on the weight scale and every single thing I ate. I held onto this picture tightly during those training years as a way to cope with the demands of preparing for the Games. It helped me get through the day-to-day struggles.

But none of this has happened. As I wake up and contemplate the upcoming day, I desperately want to be excited about a day with new opportunities, without training and all of those worries. I should be relieved that the pain in my back and the stress has lessened. But instead, I feel like an empty shell. *Why don't I feel pride and relief? Why do I feel so awful?*
I lie there in bed with my limbs so heavy they feel like they've sunk right into the mattress. And my mind is empty and tired. I'm exhausted from trying to think of something to get excited about.

My mother knocks on the door and enters my bedroom. The downward curve of her lips and the cracks in her forehead add to my sense of heaviness. As she sighs deeply, I feel her warm breath come over me.
"Where has my vibrant, self-assured daughter gone? I want her back" says my mother. "Let's go out for lunch today. We can go to our favourite restaurant. It's a beautiful warm day out there and we can eat on the patio and have fun people-watching."
Ohhhh ... the last thing I want to do is to get out of bed, get dressed, get in the car, be in public and have to talk to other people. Why does this outing, which at every other time has made me happy, now just bring a sense of dread? But I know mum is trying everything she can to make me feel better and I know she's worried about me. So, I better go ... just to try to put a smile on my mother's face.

At lunch, I review the menu carefully, paying close attention to the calorie count of each meal. I hear my coach's voice in my head: *"only salads are allowed... and no dressing."* My mother notices the time I'm taking choosing a meal.
"Don't worry, honey, no one is going to weigh you tomorrow. You can choose whatever you want to eat and don't need to worry about negative consequences now."
But her voice is very quiet compared to my coach's dominating voice in my head. I can see the weigh scale in my mind with my coach hovering

over the numbers, waiting for the magical number to appear. In the end, my coach wins again, and I choose the salad – without dressing – and my mother's frown reappears.

Partway through lunch, a friend of my mother's comes to our table to say hi.

"Congratulations on the Olympics! What an amazing accomplishment. You must be so proud. What was the experience like?"

Shit… the dreaded question. My head gets heavy, and my eyes are pulled downwards towards the placemat. I take a deep breath and tell myself to pull it together.

"It was great, thanks."

The weight of holding back the truth that the experience was a nightmare, my coaches were monsters, my back pain was all-consuming, and I barely ate, is exhausting. The Olympics is the last thing in the world I want to talk about. I feel my mother's sense of pride turn to disappointment as she knows I'm lying to her friend. Damn, now I'm feeling even worse knowing I'm making my mother unhappy. She doesn't deserve that. *Oh, please, just let me go home.*

[*Six months later*]

I've returned to school and feel good about doing something other than avoiding the world from my bedroom. For the first time in what feels like forever, I feel some sense of happiness. But there are still struggles. *How long can I keep avoiding having to explain to my classmates why I am in first year university at the age of 23? Why do I still weigh myself every day? Why do I still avoid eating carbs?*

My body has changed so much since I retired. I've gained weight and lost muscle – a bad combination that has actually made my body image worse. I don't need my coach present anymore to weigh me or to comment on my body as I still hear her voice in my head. Sometimes, my coach's voice merges with mine: *Eating carbs will make you fat… eat a smaller portion… fill up on water before eating.* I don't have a weigh scale at home anymore, but I find myself regularly pinching different areas of my body to test for extra weight. My body owns me – not the other way around.

I've been going to therapy twice a week, in a warm office that is filled with plants and the encouraging face of my therapist. My therapist tries to get me to talk about what happened:

"Tell me about your training days. What did it look like? What did it feel like?"

Oh God, really? You expect me to go there?

"It was tough" I say, "but it's tough for any athlete training for the Olympic Games. It's not supposed to be easy."

What a lame answer! I know she won't accept that response, but I don't want to get into the truth. I stare blankly at the wall, trying to think of something to say without answering her questions. To answer her questions directly and tell her about my experiences means spending extraordinary amounts of energy I don't have and sure don't want to spend this way.

"Yes, I'm sure it's tough for every Olympic hopeful but what made it especially tough for you?" she asks.

Damn, she's not going to let me get away with evading her questions! Any time I think about what happened, I can feel the heat of the tears behind my eyes. I don't want to cry about this anymore, but I know if I open my mouth to tell her the truth about my experiences, a flood of tears is inevitable. My brain says that keeping these feelings locked down is not helpful, but my gut says, *don't open up, don't open the floodgates.* I really just don't want to re-live any of it. I just want to move on. My therapist looks at me patiently, and we sit in silence seemingly in a contest to see who can wait out the silence longer.

She usually won that contest with me feeling uncomfortable with the silence and finally saying something. My therapist used those opportunities to help me disassemble the brick wall I built around my emotions – one brick at a time. Slowly, I have come to realize that people are not supposed to treat others the way that my coaches treated me and my teammates. I knew this in other walks of life, like at school or between friends, but why did it feel so normal while I was swimming? I just thought these negative experiences were normal in sport and necessary if I wanted to be the best. After all, being an Olympic level athlete is not supposed to be easy. Now, I know that the things I experienced should not be considered okay. I was surprised to learn that many of the behaviours used by my coaches are considered abusive. This was the first time I ever thought of them like that.

But the realization that I had experienced abusive coaching practices didn't bring any sense of calmness; in fact, I was hurt and angry. *Why did no one stop my coaches?* There were a lot of people watching training – therapists, psychologists, trainers – and if this was abuse, *why did no one say anything?* So now, on top of the sadness and shame I felt from my sport, I also feel anger that I was in a situation I shouldn't have been in, and adults who were supposed to protect athletes, just didn't. They must have known it was wrong so why didn't they do anything? At least I am starting to realize that my experiences weren't my fault and the way I was treated was really not acceptable.

On the plus side, I now have a boyfriend. One evening we were sitting on his couch and we started talking about my time as a swimmer. I shared some of the stories that weren't too painful, some of the stuff that I thought wasn't so bad. I remember the first time I opened up, we were sitting on the couch, cuddling, when I said: "Yeah, we used to get weighed regularly and the coaches would post everyone's weights on a white board on the pool deck so everyone could see what each other weighed. There was a lot of stress around the weighing, but it helped with self-discipline when it came to eating."

He looked at me as though I had told him someone was plotting a murder against me.

"Are you kidding me? That is outrageous. I can't believe that was ever allowed."

Taken aback, I was silent for a few seconds. I forget that these experiences aren't normal to other people, and it's nice to have people other than my therapist tell me that these experiences are not normal.

"I grew up with it and didn't know any differently, so I just thought it was normal and even though it was stressful, I thought the coaches were trying to help us be better athletes."

"Yeah, well, there have to be healthier ways of developing athletes. I can't believe you and the other athletes put up with it," he said. He continued, "what you should have done was….," telling me all the things I should have done to stop these behaviours. *If only it had been that easy!* He really doesn't understand the context or the power dynamics between elite athletes and their coaches. I don't like it when he tells me what to do. It makes me feel badly about myself and reminds me of my coaches. *It's still better than what I was used to when I was swimming,* I tell myself, *and at least I know that he loves me, don't I?*

The Long Road to Re-Building

[*Ten years later*]

I stare at the slightly stained envelope in my hands. I know what it is, and I can't believe I found it again. I remember searching for it everywhere when I moved to my new house years ago. With trembling fingers, I carefully open it, as if what I am cradling is not paper, but that tiny, fragile little thing I was after the Olympics.

My therapist gave me a final homework before the end of the therapy. She asked me to write a letter to my younger self, telling her whatever I thought would have helped me back then. I now stare at those words of encouragement, pain, love in front of me, while I hear my voice…

Dear younger me,

I have spent quite some time thinking back to those days, *your* days, and there are a few things I'd like you to know. Part of me wants to protect you, but in general I just want to let you see that life will be okay at some point, although it might seem unbearable right now. All this pain will go away and you'll feel whole and happy with yourself again at some point.

I've graduated school and am working for a sport organization, it's great to still be involved with sports in a different way. I've been able to use the skills that I have developed as an athlete – time management, organization, and goal setting – along with some new skills I learned through sport management, to excel in my new role. I love that I can give back and hopefully inspire a new generation of athletes. I finally have found a new passion and have an intense drive to build my new career.

It's taken six years, and it has been a long road, but I can definitely say I am the most confident I have ever been. It's crazy to think that I am more confident now than I was when I was standing on the pool deck waiting for my competition to start at the Olympics. I never thought confidence would be something that I needed to achieve, but it feels like one of my greatest accomplishments. I've also learned to love myself and can proudly say that out loud. I have learned that I don't need to compare myself to others to be okay with myself, and I can accept the parts of my body that were constantly scrutinized by my coaches. I realize that I don't need to be perfect to feel good enough about myself. In fact, feeling good about myself was the reason I eventually left that relationship with my boyfriend. It was not as healthy as it should have been. My acceptance of emotionally abusive behaviours in sport carried into my relationship unfortunately but at least this time I knew it was wrong.

When I think of my time as an athlete – I still get a sinking feeling, but it's less intense each time, and the feelings don't last as long. I don't think this will ever truly go away, but I have learned to accept it as part of my past. The memories sometimes come up in unexpected ways. Like last week, I went with a group of friends to a local park to play frisbee. It was a beautiful day and I could feel the warmth of the sun on my face. Playing frisbee was new to me and I loved the lightness of playing. There is no competition, no stress, and I love the way everyone just goofs around and laughs together. Then, one of my friends who likes to call everyone by their last names, was trying to get my attention to pass me the disc and called out "Zimmerman." I froze and all sense of lightness and joy vanished. I saw my coach standing on the pool deck screaming my last name, which she did every time I was in trouble. I felt small and insignificant. It's not unlike the nightmares I have frequently – it often is the same scene where I get back into the pool, and I know I am the worst one there, without a clue of what I am supposed to be doing, and can see my coach, red in the face from all of the screaming she is doing at me. I guess it's like an athlete's version of showing up to an important exam without studying.

Some of the memories are still so vivid in my mind, like the time my coach yelled at me and told me I was worthless and a waste of her time while warming up for the world championships. It lives in my mind like a picture hanging on my wall. Other times are not as vivid, but I remember the feelings that I had. I remember that feeling of my stomach turning, thinking, sometimes I even laugh about it now, because some of the things my coaches told me now seem so ridiculous and absurd, but I definitely was not laughing back then. But, just so you know, not all the memories are bad. I had a great time with my teammates and getting to travel the world and represent my country, but those bad memories are really the ones that stick out like the brightest colour in a painting.

My mental health is something that I still have to work on, especially my eating disorder. It's hard not to look in the mirror and not have my coach's voice running through my head, pointing to all of the parts of my body that are squishier than they should be. But with all of those hours in my therapist's room, talking with all those plants around me, I have learned that I don't have to act on those thoughts, even if they haven't gone away completely. I've also been able to recognize the joy and the accomplishments that came with the difficult times as part of me trying to reframe my experience, and I am happy that I am able to do that, but it still gives me a small pain in my heart when I talk about that time in my life. I know that I have to let go of a lot of the pain and anger I felt when I was an athlete, and have accepted that time in my life – it kind of just lives in a little box in my head now and I don't take it out very often.

I have accepted my experiences, grown from the anger, the sadness, and the disappointment and have become stronger and more confident over time. As much as my sport experiences have made me a stronger person, I know now that I shouldn't have had to go through many of them and no one else should have to go through what I had to. It was definitely the most difficult time of my life, and I would never want to do it again. *What will it take to make it different for today's athletes? What will it take to produce top athletes without destroying their health and spirit along the way?* These are the questions that keep my mind busy now and I'm passionate about making a difference for today's young athletes.

Anyway, younger me, stay strong. We will get through this.

Reflective Questions

1   How could the embodiment of the athletes' experiences best be described?
2   Is it possible to devote oneself fully to a sport pursuit (e.g., Olympic Games) and not have to re-build afterwards?
3   How can body composition and appearance requirements in aesthetic sports be addressed without encouraging disordered eating/eating disorders and body dysmorphia?
4   What could be done to prevent the difficulties experienced by this athlete?

References

Alexander, K., Stafford, A., & Lewis, R. (2011). *The experiences of children participating in organized sport in the UK*. The University of Edinburgh, Child Protection Research Centre.

Gervis, M., Rhind, D., & Luzar, A. (2016). Perceptions of emotional abuse in the coach–athlete relationship in youth sport: The influence of competitive level and outcome. *International Journal of Sports Science & Coaching, 11*(6), 772–779. https://doi.org/10.1177/1747954116676103

Kerr, G., & Dacyshyn, A. (2000). The retirement experiences of elite, female gymnasts. *Journal of Applied Sport Psychology, 12*(2), 115–133. https://doi.org/10.1080/10413200008404218

Kerr, G., Willson, E., & Stirling, A. (2019). *Prevalence of maltreatment among current and former national team athletes* (pp. 1–51). https://athletescan.com/sites/default/files/images/prevalence_of_maltreatment_reporteng.pdf

Kerr, G., Willson, E., & Stirling, A. (2020). "It Was the Worst Time in My Life": The effects of emotionally abusive coaching on female Canadian national team athletes. *Women in Sport and Physical Activity Journal, 28*(1), 81–89. https://doi.org/10.1123/wspaj.2019-0054

Parent, S., & Vaillancourt-Morel, M.-P. (2020). Magnitude and risk factors for interpersonal violence experienced by Canadian teenagers in the sport context. *Journal of Sport and Social Issues*, 1–17. https://doi.org/10.1177/0193723520973571

Stafford, A., Alexander, K., & Fry, D. (2015). 'There was something that wasn't right because that was the only place I ever got treated like that': Children and young people's experiences of emotional harm in sport. *Childhood, 22*(1), 121–137. https://doi.org/10.1177/0907568213505625

Stirling, A. E., & Kerr, G. A. (2008). Defining and categorizing emotional abuse in sport. *European Journal of Sport Science, 8*(4), 173–181. https://doi.org/10.1080/17461390802086281

Stirling, A. E., & Kerr, G. A. (2013). The perceived effects of elite athletes' experiences of emotional abuse in the coach–athlete relationship. *International Journal of Sport and Exercise Psychology, 11*(1), 87–100. https://doi.org/10.1080/1612197X.2013.752173

Vertommen, T., Schipper-van Veldhocken, N., Wouters, K., Kampen, J. K., Brackenridge, C., Rhind, D., … Van Den Eede, F. (2016). Interpersonal violence against children in sport in the Netherlands and Belgium. *Child Abuse & Neglect, 51*, 223–236. https://doi.org/10.1016/j.chiabu.2015.10.006

Part III
Moving Beyond "Just" Creative Nonfiction

10 Learning the Craft
Confessions on Writing Creative Nonfiction

Francesca Cavallerio and Ross Wadey

Introduction

In recent years, scholars have encouraged the use of a variety of methods of data collection, analysis, and representation when engaging in qualitative research (McGannon, Smith, Kendellen, & Gonsalves, 2019). In response to this call, this book aimed to provide examples of how a specific type of creative analytical practice (CAP), creative nonfiction (CNF), can be used as a different way to represent and communicate research. By adopting literary techniques and a narrative writing style (Goodall, 2019), CNF allows researchers to reach a wider audience and – potentially – ensure their research has an impact on the communities they conduct their studies *with* and *for*. Nonetheless, while the hope is that this text inspires the reader to adopt this form of representation, it might also still appear "scary" and "out of reach" for others. When inviting authors to contribute to this book, not everyone jumped at the chance to embrace CNF. While a few rejections were due to lack of time and prior engagements, many were not brave enough to take a leap into the unknown (e.g., "I'm a scientist, not a novelist"). To dampen the concerns of future scholars and facilitate the uptake of this creative analytical practice, this chapter aims to lift the veil of the authors' experiences of writing CNF and the lessons they have learnt along the way.

The purpose of this chapter therefore is twofold: first is to present the reader with confessions on the process of writing CNF. To do so, we sent the authors in this book a survey on their experiences of writing CNF for the first time and analysed it using reflexive thematic analysis (Braun & Clarke, 2019). Second is to represent the analysis of these confessions through the medium of two different tales, realist and CNF. We asked ourselves what could have been the most useful way to represent our findings. Could we go beyond 'simply' reporting the themes identified in our analysis? Could this chapter provide a 'practice space' itself? The answers to these questions can be found in the following sections. First, we present a table that shows the result of our analysis, including quotes that were deemed representatives of our themes (Table 10.1). Then we present a realist tale of the findings, followed by a CNF. A final reflection and a few questions close the chapter.

DOI: 10.4324/9781003038900-14

Table 10.1 Results and data extracts from our reflexive thematic analysis

Theme	Definition	Example quotes
Learning the craft	This theme illuminates the challenges authors face when writing CNF. From technical aspects (e.g., when is a story 'good enough'?), to ethical ones (e.g., where is the line between representing data creatively and imagining things?), to the practicalities of writing.	"I first spent time trying to work out what approach would be the most evocative and best way to communicate the findings - one character, multiple characters, etc. Then I focused upon how I might articulate the different components of this character and the experiences that she wanted to portray" "using some of our own thoughts and feelings to construct a basic structure from which we could weave the data from the original article into" "I then combined that with the typical idea that all stories should have a 'beginning middle and end' to come up with a rough structure for the story, and listed the main characters with a brief description of their biographies" "Make sure you have a clear storyboard, know where you want to start, where you want to finish and what you want to communicate in between" "Knowing when to stop, what to tweak, and how much information I needed" "I found myself getting quite invested in the story and I wanted to make sure it was perfect, which is of course, impossible." "I found that I was continually wrestling with the question, 'what blend of creativity compared to nonfiction constitutes good CNF writing?'" "Being able to get the important theoretical messages across clearly without losing these in description / contextual information that is obviously important for the story to make sense but is not so important in a theoretical sense." "The confidence to know if what I was producing was 'good enough'."
A relational process and product	The theme highlights how the experience of writing a CNF contains in itself different layers of 'sharing': it provides a new opportunity	"I shared my chapter with Fran, as I was keen to gain thoughts and also because I was really enjoying the writing process and wanted to see what other people thought. Obviously, the chapter was shared with my co-author Chris for thoughts and input and once I finished it, I shared it with my mum" "As a team we work extremely well and having two people in the team passionate about the sport we were focusing on, plus Jaqui pushing and probing us for even more evocative words or stories it really made the whole process very enjoyable indeed." "I shared it with a friend and listened to her responses, edited it slightly then sent to Fran as a first draft."

| A relational process and product | for creating an embodied sense of participants' experience, involving the writer firstly with the data, to then expand to a sense of collaboration within the writing team/friends asked for feedback, and finally reaching out to the audience, creating a connection. | *"I also enjoyed thinking back to what it was like doing the research itself (collecting data in situ) and bringing those aspects into my story and the descriptions within."*
 "Writing this Chapter involved re-engaging with the dataset I had originally published and used to frame the subsequent work. Instantly, the extracts from the reflexive journal brought back the gritty reality of 'doing' the fieldwork."
 "as a mechanism to enable those researchers to realise their 'subjects' are actually human with rich, varied and worthwhile experiences of the phenomena they collect data on"
 "CNFs in the form of first-person stories don't have to be the end product! They can be an analytical activity that helps you to make sense of your participants before you start to 'deconstruct' experiences through other analytical methods"
 "I think it is a powerful tool to bring situations, scenarios, thoughts and feelings to life. And not just to life but to connect them to the real world."
 "once I finished it, I shared it with my mum. I think it's the first piece of work I have shared with her but given the topic and the way in which it was written I thought she would find it interesting." |
| Letting the academic breathe | This theme portrays the (positive) experience of academics engaging with a different type of writing: different from the usual highly regulated forms of scientific writing, CNF allowed academics to feel their voice was let out freely. | *"I laughed as I wrote some sections of it but also found myself getting quite emotional thinking about the original interviews underpinning the story as well as my own experiences. It's definitely the most emotional writing experience I've had but also the most enjoyable by a very long way."*
 "Hopefully, readers will feel immersed in the events and, as the observer, a bit powerless in the face of events they might not approve of."
 "I found it gave me a voice that I wasn't aware that I had"
 "There are fewer rules in creative nonfiction"
 "I have thoroughly enjoyed re-engaging with the original dataset to emphasise, re-cast, and re-imagine some new possibilities with the representation. This has been an emotive task that has forced me to (re)consider the competing roles I occupied within the ethnography, and the subsequent roles I continue to negotiate"
 "I liked that it brought me back to a bit more of a 'childhood' type approach to writing, as I used to really enjoy writing stories as a child."
 "I felt liberated by the 'creative' element to re-write, re-frame and explore new characters, experiences and settings that previously had not previously been presented." |

Confessions of Engaging with CNF for the First Time: A Realist Tale

Three themes were identified as a result of the reflexive thematic analysis. These were (a) 'Letting the Academic Breathe,' (b) 'Learning the Craft,' and (c) 'A Relational Process and Product.'

Letting the Academic Breathe

This theme portrays the sense of freedom elicited through the creative writing experience and how the experience opened new possibilities with data. To contextualize this theme, sport and exercise researchers have traditionally always been *prescribed* how to represent their research. For example, the Sixth Edition of the American Psychological Association (APA) Publication Manual (2010) provides over 400 pages of guidance on how to submit a manuscript for publication in accordance with their specific style. Given that most journals align with these APA guidelines, academics have by-and-large adhered to this conventional scientific form of writing, representing their research in this dominant scientific way. Yet, while this conventional mode of representation is well respected and has made a major contribution in various fields of research, there have been repeated calls to open up new possibilities for alternative forms of representation (e.g., Denzin & Lincoln, 2000; McMahon, 2017; Sparkes, 2002; Van Maanen, 1988).

Against this backdrop, and from reflecting on and making comparisons with their experiences of using the dominant scientific form of representation, the contributing authors expressed a sense of freedom from engaging with creative nonfiction and how it gave them a voice, a noticeable shift from the 'shackles' of convention. One author reported how they found that "There are fewer rules with creative nonfiction. Less emphasis on short and concise sentences and euphemistic language. Evoking emotion through words loaded with feeling and poise was freeing." The opportunity to engage in this creative analytical practice also opened new possibilities with data: "I felt liberated by the creative element; to rewrite, re-frame, and explore new characters, experiences and settings that had not previously been presented." This quote would appear to align with Laurel Richardson's (2000) thinking when she reported, "Writing is also a way of 'knowing' – a method of discovery and analysis. By writing in different ways, we discover new aspects of our topic and our relationship to it" (p. 293). To elaborate here, the authors felt that creative nonfiction enabled them to more effectively convey the *richness* and *complexity* in their original dataset that they felt were restricted by conventional scientific practice. One author reported, "It allowed for a better insight into how the different themes identified in the original study were interacting and being experienced at the same time, which I felt was missing in the original study." Other authors reported how it connected participants and context, "In presenting this work as creative nonfiction, I hope that the chapter builds upon the original studies by sparking interest in the unseen and often ignored backstage of athletes' everyday practices," as well as with the real world: "I think [creative nonfiction] is a powerful tool to bring situations, scenarios, thoughts, and feelings to life. And not just to life but to connect them to the real world."

Learning the Craft

The theme reflects the *how* or the process of *doing* creative writing. From the outset, the authors were given the freedom to engage with creative nonfiction as they saw fit. After all, a 'one size fits all approach' would misalign with and downplay the creativity of this creative analytic practice. That said, this freedom and ultimately the novelty of the experience was met with a certain degree of trepidation by the authors: How do I start? How do I structure the story? How do I develop the characters? How do I communicate the story? Is this a 'good' story? These questions put a halt to writing. One author reported, "I found that I was continuing wrestling with the question, 'what blend of creativity compared to non-fiction constitutes good CNF writing?'" Another expressed, "I first spent time trying to work out what approach would be the most evocative and the best way to communicate the findings – one character vs. multiple characters etc." What was evident from the authors' confessions was that a lot of forethought was required *before* the writing could commence.

Early considerations by the authors included the structure of the story, character development, striking the 'right' balance between contextual information and theoretical messages, and ensuring the story did not betray the context originally studied. One author reported how for them, "… all stories should have a beginning, middle, and end" and how they "… listed the main characters with a brief description of their biographies." Yet, even following this forethought, the authors expressed how the writing experience was iterative, dynamic, and reflexive. It was a process of trial and error and going back and forth with their datasets, reflexive notes, and/or original article(s). One author expressed how the stories, "… reflect hours and hours of analytical work to piece events together, and hours of deliberation about what should or shouldn't be included, or how things should or shouldn't be written."

One crucial element of the writing experience that resonated across the participants' reflections was how they were personally invested and how they found the experience to be confessional, emotional, and pleasurable. To elaborate, the authors reflected how they became part of the writing process; how they drew upon their own thoughts, feelings, reflexive notes, experiences, and imaginations to construct their story. Two authors reported,

> Having been a swimmer myself, as was Adam, and currently still working within a competitive swimming setting as a coach I/we was/ were able to draw upon a significant amount of personal embodied knowledge about competitive swimming. ... Our CNF therefore became somewhat confessional, using some of our own thoughts and feelings to construct a basic structure from which we could weave the data from the original article into

and

> My favourite bands are The Lumineers, Muse, and Florence + the Machine. Very different music. But the lead singers all evoke deep feelings in me. When I write, I try to do the same. If I feel the same way as I do when I listen and hear their songs, then I know my voice is coming out.

Throughout the writing experience, the authors also expressed how they found it enjoyable and pleasurable: "I liked that it brought me back to a bit more of a 'childhood' type approach to writing, as I used to really enjoy writing stories as a child." Another expressed, "I found myself getting quite emotional thinking about the original interviews underpinning the story as well as my own experiences. It's the most emotional writing experience I've had but also the most enjoyable by a very long way."

A Relational Process and Product

This theme expresses how the creative writing experience was a *shared* experience in its construction (e.g., between authors and participants and with co-authors) and communication with readers. For example, it was expressed how the writing experience enabled the authors to reconnect with their participants; it provided an alternative way to re-analyse, know, and gain an embodied sense of the participants' experiences. Indeed, the authors expressed that creative nonfiction doesn't *just* have to be a form of representation; it can also provide researchers with a novel analytical activity to make sense of participants' experiences before proceeding with other methods of analysis. One author reported,

> ... first-person stories don't have to be the end-product! They can be an analytical activity that helps to make sense of your participants before you start to 'deconstruct' experiences through other analytical methods. In other words, sometimes you need to put the story together and see the whole before you can make sense of its parts.

The writing process was also shared between co-authors. Some authors reported how their co-author, "... pushed and probed us for even more evocative words or stories" and how, "... it really made the whole process very enjoyable." It was recommended by the authors to get critical friends to read one's stories and to welcome feedback from them: Does it move them? Does it evoke emotion? Does it resonate with them? Does it capture their attention? What's missing? What's the take-home message? Does the story 'hang' together? Would they share it? Who would they share it with? One author reported, "I found discussions with the Editor (Francesca) invaluable to consider how I was developing characters, settings, and the overall plot." Another expressed, "Jaqui as the non-swimmer was then able to ask the naïve questions to check and challenge Adam and I in terms of what we meant by certain terms or thoughts or feelings." Here, the use of co-authors aligns with the process of 'critical friends' to enhance the rigour of qualitative research, which is a "a process of critical dialogue between people, with researchers giving voice to their interpretation in relation to other people who listen and offer critical feedback" (Smith & McGannon, 2018, p. 113). The role of the critical friends is not to agree or achieve consensus but rather to encourage reflexivity.

Unlike their original articles that were written by academics for academics, the authors also expressed how they wanted to share the final product with others about the multiple realities of those who participate in sport and exercise. As Sparkes and Smith (2014) wrote, "Conducting qualitative research is not just a private affair conducted for the enjoyment of the researcher. The results or findings of the study need to be conveyed to others" (p. 147). One participant expressed, "Once I had finished it, I shared it with my Mum. I think it's the first piece of work I have shared with her." Furthermore, the stories were considered a useful way to communicate their research with their intended audiences (e.g., athletes, coaches, practitioners, students): "I have shared these stories and collected reader's responses—it's fascinating to see the way people interact with these stories differently and draw different conclusions about the "goodness" of the characters." Importantly, it was felt that these stories might stimulate reflection, dialogue, and perhaps social change: "To quote Robin Williams, words and ideas can change the world. I do not believe that my chapter will change the world, but if we don't try then, I believe, we are just wasting time putting squiggly lines together."

Confessions of Engaging with CNF for the First Time: A Creative Nonfiction

Perfect! Look at this, isn't this perfect? I tell myself, appreciating the space around me in the café. *I love sitting on these stools by the window, so much natural light coming in and...*

'Your mocha'

'Thank you!'

...and a lovely mocha to get started.

Today is going to be a good day. Today I will write. I know it. Today I will sip my coffee, let my gaze wander for a couple of minutes among the students speeding around on their bikes. I will breathe in, being mindful of my body, cleaning my mind, and let the music transport me into a writing daze.

[Ten minutes later]

No way! How can these possibly be out of charge?

I take the Air Pods out of my ears, look at them in disbelief...I am sure I charged them throughout the night, I always do when I have a café writing session. I can't work without music in a café!

I put them back in their case and snap it shut. Useless!

What do I do now? I can't go back home, I'll waste too much time, I have another appointment here in two hours. And I need to write. The example of creative nonfiction our lecturer gave us to write for the Research Methods module is due tomorrow and I only have my title page ready.

My head falls in my hands, shoulders sagging.

How can she want us to do something like this? I don't get it. Why can't we just write a lab report, or do something on SPSS? I am a sport scientist, I don't need to be able to write stories, I need to be able to write proper science, to explain athletes and coaches about science.

And even if they liked a story – a story, COME ON! – How am I supposed to do that? I am no writer! I have the results she gave us from her study. Themes and quotes, and descriptions, definitions... It makes perfect sense the way it is, why would someone change it? We are academics, not writers. And what does 'creative nonfiction' even mean? Either something is creative, or it is not. And science shouldn't be creative. Science is science. If we start telling stories, how will people know what is true?

'Hello! So lovely to see you again!'

The rant in my head suddenly stops.

U-oh...I know this voice.

'Hi! It is! Finally! This coffee was really long due.'

I am like a statue. *How many people were in the café when I walked in? Surely, she won't notice me, right?*

Still holding my head in my hands, I peak through my fingers to check the corner where I hear the voices coming from. It's her. *No way! Have I just conjured her up while moaning about the assignment she gave us?*

'Shall we sit down there, near those big windows?'

NO!

'Yes, there is so much light, it's perfect'

Please don't see me, please don't see me, I don't want to talk to you right now.

The screeching of a chair behind me makes me realise they stopped at the table just before me. *She hasn't seen me.*

'Cappuccino?'

'For me, please.'

Ok, she must be sitting closer to me, so her back is to me and she can't see me. Pheeew. I remove my head from the hands, take a deep breath, and sit poised to write at the laptop, as if willing my fingers to write the assignment for me.

'So...how was it? Did you hate me for inviting you to write that chapter? I felt so guilty to do that in the middle of a pandemic!'

...I want my Air Pods back. I want them in my ears. How will I ever write a single word with her voice here? I don't want to listen to her conversation with her colleague...

'Are you joking? I loved it! It was like a ray of light during those months...a respite from admin, emails, teaching, teaching, emails, admin!'

'Haha, really? That's such a relief! So, what did you enjoy about the process?

'All of it! I really enjoyed writing this story and have definitely been sold on creative nonfiction as an approach for representing findings. I loved having the freedom to be creative, while grounding the story in data. I found it gave me a voice that I wasn't aware that I had, as well as allowing me to amplify the voices of my participants far more. I really liked that I could bring ideas to life so much more than I am usually able to within studies.'

...creative nonfiction? Have I heard correctly? Are they talking about my nightmare assignment? I find myself leaning back into the chair and slouching down slightly, as if that somehow makes me and my eavesdropping invisible. I keep my hands on the keyboard to show that I'm writing, not eavesdropping, but also just in case they say something that I can use for my assignment.

'I'm so glad to hear this! I mean, you know me, I love this type of writing, so when I realised it was a possibility, for me it was almost like hearing something click, fall into place. It's perfect to do research in my area, with non-experts and with children.'

...yeah, I've heard this before... "creative nonfiction is a great way to share research findings with non-academic audiences,[1] *blah blah blah"...*

'Yes, and I can really see why now! I mean, I shared the chapter with my mum! I think it's the first piece of work I have shared with her but, you know, given the topic and the way in which it was written I thought she would find it interesting. And she loved it!'

'I am not surprised, I absolutely loved it too! As soon as you sent it to me, I started reading – I was so curious – and I felt so immersed in everything that was going on.'

'I'm really glad you think so. But the funny thing is that it was the same for me, while writing! I laughed as I wrote some sections of it but also found myself getting quite emotional thinking about the original interviews underpinning the story as well as my own experiences. It's definitely the most emotional writing experience I've had but also the most enjoyable by a very long way.'

...aw, this is interesting. So, she's writing – no, not writing...editing – a book on this stuff? If someone is publishing a book then, maybe it's more than just something only she likes to do. And this colleague seems to really like it too. I take a sip from my coffee, sit back in the chair, and cradle the cup in my hands.

'And you know, it might sound funny, but I really liked that it brought me back to a bit more of a "childhood" type approach to writing. I used to really enjoy writing stories as a child. I felt liberated by the "creative" element to re-write, re-frame, and explore new characters, experiences, and settings that had not been presented in the published realist tale.'

'Sounds like you just completely, utterly loved the whole process. Any challenges?'

...yeah, the blank page staring at you...

'Well, now...of course there were some...let's call them 'scary bits' while writing'

... and what were these scary bits?

'And what were these scary bits?'

'Well, to start with, the confidence to know if what I was producing was "good enough". I found myself getting quite invested in the story and I wanted to make sure it was perfect, which is of course, impossible.'

...I've got no chance. I'm no writer, I can't do this.

'And then there was that constant feeling, like a need to achieve balance, to make sure I wasn't betraying the readers. I found that I was continually wrestling with the question, "what blend of creativity compared to nonfiction constitutes good CNF writing?"'

...well, at least my doubts were not totally stupid. I mean, if you 'create,' then you are not reporting your data. How is that ethical?

'That is such a good point! I had a student last week who brought up exactly this point, "how can readers trust research then, where is the line?"'

Ah...that would be me. I feel myself wincing. *She must hate me.*

'It was a really great discussion, you know. She is a smart one, and her questions encouraged me to look more into this.'

Aw. Really? Thanks. I replace the coffee cup on the table and rest my hands in my lap.

'It is challenging, because often creative nonfiction is discussed as literary or journalistic style, and not everything can be linked to research. But I think – in relation to your point, I liked Kara's idea[2] that researchers need to maintain a reflexive awareness of the details they include and exclude, and of the possible consequences of their decision. I believe there is no recipe on the blend, as you said, I don't think we can say "have 60% of data and mix it with 40% of creativity" ... each story, each research project, is unique and if we try to encapsulate and rule creative writing, then where does the creativity go? My conclusion – if this helps you in anyway – is that it's more linked to Barone and Eisner's[3] idea of arts-based research as a way to create *metanarratives* that challenge what they call *master narratives*, those finalising narratives that seem to tell us what is right and what is wrong, and how we need to think. If in our research representation we are able to mix conflicting perspectives – at times creating characters in order to ensure a master narrative is represented – without aiming for a tone of finality, an overpowering researcher's voice, then I think ethically we are on the right way.'

Wow. She did take note of my question. This sounds quite interesting actually…although I still wonder how scientific research can be considered seriously if it is fictional.[4]

'That's a really interesting point, thanks. It does help…or at least it's encouraging! You know, it's so challenging this whole idea of stories being out of our control,[5] so the closer the publication date, the more nervous I get. I mean, sharing these stories with others! Because of my research philosophy, I feel a deep ownership over the stories…what if readers don't get them? What if I wasn't able to get the important theoretical messages across clearly without losing these in contextual information? I mean, that is obviously important for the story to make sense but is not so important in a theoretical sense.'

'I remember this was your worry from the beginning. And it makes perfect sense. I actually think it makes your story better, because you thought about it. Trust me, I asked myself these questions throughout the editing of the book, and every time I write a CNF. When I wrote my first story, I remember Professor Rossi telling me, "Emma, gaining a sense of 'how' the representation will be read is a crucial aspect of developing the story. I know this can be a vulnerable process, but my advice is to always expose your writing to critical feedback." And I know you have done this, you told me yourself.'

'I did. You are right. I should stop worrying. I shared it with a friend and listened to her responses, edited it slightly, and obviously I shared with my co-author for thoughts and input. As a team, we work extremely well and being both passionate about the sport we were focusing on helped, then having you pushing and probing us for even more evocative words or stories… it really made the whole process enjoyable, indeed. And you know what? It's not just about the readers, to be honest. I also enjoyed thinking back to what it was like doing the research itself and bringing those aspects into my story and the descriptions within. Instantly, the extracts from the reflexive journal brought back the gritty reality of "doing" the fieldwork. I think we should consider writing research as CNF not only something for *others*, but possibly also as a mechanism to enable researchers to realise their "subjects" are actually human with rich, varied, and worthwhile experiences of the phenomena they collect data on.'

'This is such a great point. CNF as a way to re-humanise research data. Listen, I was thinking of organising a research seminar for the students in my qualitative research lab on creative nonfiction…would you like to join? You could present a confessional tale of your experience of writing the chapter? Maybe telling them a bit more about the process of 'learning the craft of CNF'?'

Sigh, I wish this talk had been organised today. Maybe I'd have a chance to get my head around and produce something. I wonder if this person would share her wisdom with me…like a preview?

"I would love to. I mean, I only wrote one, so I won't be banking on a huge amount of experience…'

'That's perfect. It makes it more relatable to them. Funny, my Research Methods students have a deadline tomorrow and I asked them to write a creative nonfiction. I bet they'd love to listen to your experience!'

…indeed, they would. I'd be over the moon even having done it once!

'Wow, that's quite a challenge. I remember feeling a bit at a loss at the beginning, not sure where and how to start…'

'…and how did you start, then?'

Exactly my question. Thank you for asking.

'I made a plan. I think you need to make sure you have a clear storyboard, know where you want to start, where you want to finish, and what you want to communicate in between. I first spent time trying to work out what approach would be the most evocative and best way to communicate the findings – one character, multiple characters, etc. Then I focused upon how I might articulate the different components of this character and the experiences that she wanted to portray. I came up with a rough structure for the story and listed the main characters with a brief description of their biographies. Once I got started, the challenge wasn't writing anymore, instead it became knowing when to stop, what to tweak, and how much information I needed. I have thoroughly enjoyed re-engaging with the original dataset to emphasise, re-cast, and re-imagine some new possibilities with the representation. I think it is a powerful tool to bring situations, scenarios, thoughts, and feelings to life. And not just to life but to connect them to the real world.'

Mm. Listening to these two being so enthusiastic makes me almost want to try again. Maybe there is a chance I can try and do this? She is just making it sound like a nice experience, actually. And it actually sounds interesting. I reach for my coffee, take a sip, and look at my screen.

'It is definitely a powerful tool, yes. And you know what? I think editing this book and having conversations with all the authors of the chapters, listening to their experiences, gave me a chance to understand – possibly – the famous quote by Laurel Richardson, writing as a level of analysis.[6] I know it's a classic quote, but it only ever made sense in theory, not so much in practice. After spending so much time thinking about, and discussing CNF, I can see how it also allows for a better insight into how different themes identified in the original studies might be interacting and being experienced at the same time, which I feel can be missed when they are presented distinctly.'

'Absolutely. CNFs in the form of first-person stories don't have to be the end product! They can be an analytical activity that helps you make sense of your participants before you start to "deconstruct" experiences through other analytical methods.'

'I agree. We shouldn't portray it as something peculiar, it can be such a powerful tool on so many levels. I want to see students being routinely exposed to CNF as a way to help them understand topics they are studying, and for students to be taught about how to use or do CNF in ways that make them see it as a viable and valued method for developing knowledge as part of any independent research project they may have to conduct. Just one more tool. A resource. Not something weird, scary, or worse "not scientific," "not academic." There is so much potential.'

'Indeed. Let's see how your students get on with their assignment tomorrow!'

'Yeah, let's wait and see. But now, enough talking about work. Tell me how your life has been. Any news?'

Ok. Time to stop listening now. Let me go back to the assignment brief...
My eyes focus on the screen in front of me again. I down the dregs of the coffee in the cup, shake off the hands, and get typing.

Concluding (or Opening) Thoughts

Writing this chapter was challenging. We wanted to tell the tale of the authors' confessions about engaging with CNF for the first time. The data collected through the survey was rich and informative – the perks of doing qualitative research with people who understand qualitative research themselves – and we found ourselves debating what the best way to represent the findings was. Should we make sure all the themes were clearly discussed, to avoid readers missing any aspect we deemed important? Or should we story our findings, in line with the rest of the book, to allow the reader to emotionally connect with the challenges and the joys of writing CNF? We decided we wanted both things. We wanted to be able to discuss the themes identified, which we thought would be of interest and useful to the reader, and we wanted the confessions of the authors to empathically resonate with the readers' experiences. The question was, were we allowed to have both aspects in one place? Could we have a mixed representation, part realist tale and part creative nonfiction?

During the recent ECR and Student Conference of the International Society for Qualitative Research in Sport and Exercise, attendees engaged in a critical debate on CNF. Interestingly, the majority of the conversation revolved around sharing stories, with a general feeling that published CNF on peer-reviewed, academic journals "still had to be 'constrained' in the journals' limits/standard/formats" (K. Tamminen, personal communication, April 8, 2021). While over the years other examples of creative analytical practices seem to have been able to 'break free' from academic constraints, and still be published (albeit only in some journals; e.g., Henson, 2017; O'Connell & Lynch, 2020; Richardson, 1994), when it comes to CNF as a representation of research findings – versus a literary product in itself – they still end up 'buried' half-way through a standard research article, in between methods and discussion. Is it possible that this way of publishing CNF as research is impacting the choice of using it to represent a study's results? On the other hand, would it be wrong for a researcher wanting to use both methods of representation, to possibly gain from the strengths of a realist tale and of a CNF? Many ethnographers started to write their studies as realist tales, to then also publish a more confessional article (Van Maanen, 1988), so why not consider a pluralistic approach to representation of findings, along the lines of methodological pluralism (Frost & Nolas, 2011)?

We hope these questions might help to push towards new boundaries of representation, challenging normally accepted stereotypes in academic writing and ensuring research is represented in the format that most effectively portrays its findings and helps achieve its aims.

Notes

1 Smith et al. (2016).
2 Kara (2015).
3 Barone and Eisner (2011).
4 Banks and Banks (1998).
5 Frank (2010).
6 Richardson and Adams St. Pierre (2018).

References

American Psychological Association. (2010). *Publication manual of the APA* (6th ed.). Washington, DC: Author.

Banks, A., & Banks, S. P. (1998). The struggle over facts and fictions. In S. P. Banks (Ed.), *Fiction and social research: By ice or fire* (pp. 11–29). Walnut Creek, CA: AltaMira.

Barone, T., & Eisner, E. W. (2011). *Arts based research*. Thousand Oaks, CA: Sage.

Braun, V., & Clarke, V. (2019). Reflecting on reflexive thematic analysis. *Qualitative Research in Sport, Exercise and Health, 11*(4), 589–597.

Denzin, N. K., & Lincoln, Y. (Eds.). (2000). *Handbook of qualitative research* (2nd ed.). Thousand Oaks, CA: Sage.

Frank, A. W. (2010). *Letting stories breathe: A socio-narratology.* Chicago, IL: University of Chicago Press.

Frost, N. A., & Nolas, S. M. (2011). Exploring and expanding on pluralism in qualitative research in psychology. *Qualitative Research in Psychology, 8*(2), 115–119. https://doi.org/10.1080/14780887.2011.572728

Goodall Jr, H. L. (2019). *Writing qualitative inquiry: Self, stories, and academic life.* Abingdon: Routledge.

Henson, D. F. (2017). Fragments and fictions: An autoethnography of past and possibility. *Qualitative Inquiry, 23*(3), 222–224. https://doi.org/10.1177/1077800416640307

Kara, H. (2015). *Creative research methods in the social sciences: A practical guide.* Bristol: Policy Press.

McGannon, K. R., Smith, B., Kendellen, K., & Gonsalves, C. A. (2019). Qualitative research in six sport and exercise psychology journals between 2010 and 2017: An updated and expanded review of trends and interpretations. *International Journal of Sport and Exercise Psychology*, 1–21. https://doi.org/10.1080/1612197X.2019.1655779

McMahon, J. (2017). Creative analytical practices. In B. Smith & A. C. Sparkes (Eds.), *Routledge handbook of qualitative research in sport and exercise* (pp. 302–315). Abingdon: Routledge.

O'Connell, N. P., & Lynch, T. (2020). Translating deaf culture: An ethnodrama. *Qualitative Inquiry, 26*(3–4), 411–421. https://doi.org/10.1177/1077800419843945

Richardson, L. (1994). Nine poems: Marriage and the family. *Journal of Contemporary Ethnography, 23*(1), 3–13. https://doi.org/10.1177/089124194023001001

Richardson, L. (2000). Writing: A method of inquiry. In N. Denzin & Y. Lincoln (Eds.), *Handbook of qualitative research* (2nd ed.). Thousand Oaks, CA: Sage.

Richardson, L., & St. Pierre, E. A. (2018). Writing: A method of inquiry. In N. Denzin & Y. Lincoln (Eds.), *Handbook of qualitative research* (5th ed., pp. 818–838). Thousand Oaks, CA: Sage.

Smith, B., & McGannon, K. R. (2018). Developing rigor in qualitative research: Problems and opportunities within sport and exercise psychology. *International Review of Sport and Exercise Psychology, 11*(1), 101–121. https://doi.org/10.1080/1750984X.2017.1317357

Smith, B., McGannon, K. R., & Williams, T. L. (2016). Ethnographic creative nonfiction. In G. Molnár & L. Purdy (Eds.), *Ethnographies in sport and exercise research* (pp. 49–73). Abingdon: Routledge.

Sparkes, A. C. (2002). *Telling tales in sport and physical activity: A qualitative journey.* Champaign, IL: Human Kinetics Press.

Sparkes, A. C., & Smith, B. (2014). *Qualitative research methods in sport, exercise and health.* New York: Routledge.

Van Maanen, J. (1988). *Tales of the field: On writing ethnography.* Chicago, IL: University of Chicago Press.

11 Exploring Visual Storytelling as a Vehicle for Creative Nonfiction

Rebecca Palmer and Francesca Cavallerio

Introduction

Turning to arts-based methods in an attempt to impact the world we live in, raising awareness and encouraging discussion and change, are not new concepts when they appear in the last chapter of a book dedicated to creative nonfiction as a way to represent research. Yet even those researchers open to writing creative nonfiction might agree with Crane-Williams' words when she mentions, "[...] rarely does it *[research]* seem to change the way they perceive the world" (2012, p. 88). This is because the type of creative nonfiction described in the previous ten chapters is based on the written word. As much as it can be powerful and evocative, written stories might still encounter barriers (Thomas, 2012) and might – at times – still hold researchers from feeling their work is having an impact.

The aim of this final chapter, therefore, is not to bring to a close the topic of creative nonfiction – as if that could ever really be possible – but it is to leave you, Reader, with a new open door. So far, we only talked about creative nonfiction thinking of written stories, but creative nonfiction does not have to stop there. Nonfiction comics, for example, offer another possibility as a form for storytelling that uses the combined power of words and images.

In this chapter, we – Becky and I – will take you through our experience of "translating" a written creative nonfiction into a comic. Just like Crane-Williams (2012), I was looking for a new way to use my research on overuse injuries in gymnasts. The story I had written (Cavallerio et al., 2016) was proving useful to engage coaches and parents in conversation, but it was not really helpful with the young gymnasts I wanted to reach. It was still too much due to their young age. The written word and the literary techniques that worked so well in writing the creative nonfiction itself seemed to be somehow a barrier to engage the exact community my research wanted to help (Gair & Van Luyn, 2016).

"You should find someone who can make a comic out of your story. That would be a good way to share your work with gymnasts," said my

DOI: 10.4324/9781003038900-15

supervisor towards the end of my PhD. His words, as it often happens, inspired me and I started researching arts-based methods, appreciating the way they reduced the 'weight' of the written word, allowing other means of communication to give voice to often silenced populations (Foster, 2012). Nonfiction comics are a way to give visibility – literally – to silenced populations and silenced social issues (Weber, 2008). Just as the roots of creative nonfiction are linked with New Journalism (see Introduction), nonfiction comics developed on the shoulders of comics journalism, a current that acknowledges the subjectivity of the recording eye and hand and attempts to tell a more in-depth story (Weber & Rall, 2017). Nonfiction comics use constructed images to tell a story based on rigorously gathered data (Galman, 2009); therefore, it also provides a powerful medium to represent qualitative research.

What follows is a collaborative autoethnographic creative nonfiction (Ellis, 2004; Hackley, 2007) that illustrates the process of developing the "translation" of the written CNF, based on my ethnographic study, into a visual story. Each of the sections highlights a particular aspect of the process of collaboration that opened our eyes to the differences between a written CNF and its visual translation. By presenting the process as a story, it was our intention to create a sense of what such a collaboration is like as it is evolving. We hope that it captures how the meeting of different specialisms through the relationship of collabora-tors opens up new ideas and new ways of framing what was familiar to each of us.

From Words to Drawings: Stories from Our Journey

Visualising the story

[September 2019]

From: Palmer, Becky

To: Cavallerio, Francesca

Hi Fran,
Good to meet you on Tuesday, thanks again for your presentation! It would be great to meet up again to talk about this and ideas for communicating research – I'm very curious to hear about them. I'm available any time on Monday or Tuesday if either would suit you?
All the best,
Becky

From: Cavallerio, Francesca

To: Palmer, Becky

Hi Becky,
I hope you are doing well. It was really
lovely to meet you last week too. I am still
so excited at the idea of collaborating on
"translating" my story into a comic! Would
this time work for you to meet next Tuesday?
Shall we meet in Signorelli's? Good coffee and
I think it's halfway between our offices. :)
Best wishes
Fran

From: Palmer, Becky

To: Cavallerio, Francesca

Hi Fran,
Yes, that works for me - look forward to
seeing you then!
All the best
Becky

***

[sounds of dishware clinking in the background]

Fran's teaspoon circles rhythmically in the little espresso cup on the table in front of her, while she listens to Becky's thoughts on her story. It's just so exciting, she cannot even believe this is finally happening. She and Ross have been talking about turning the story into a comic to actually do something with it, use it with gymnasts, *really* try and prevent injuries. *Really* try and change the gymnastics culture, as her hashtag always says.

"...one thing I'll need to do is spend some time making drawings and collecting reference material. Do you think that it would be possible? Are there gymnastics squads that train in Cambridge, or coaches you're in touch with? Maybe they'll allow me to attend some training sessions?"

"Oh yes, of course! I can ask the club I work with in London. Would London work for you? And if you want, I can send you videos and stuff, in the meanwhile?"

"Aw, yes! That would be really useful. It would help me start picturing the scenes."

***

From: Palmer, Becky

To: Cavallerio, Francesca

Hi Fran!

These are amazing to watch – I can't get over
the group routine with the hoops, how much coordination is involved (and for the individual
routines too). Incredible! I love the ribbon
routine too… interesting what choices of music
they go for also.

I was so inspired after watching the videos,
that I had to start sketching. Attached is
a first draft (see Figure 11.1) I did of the
initial scene in the story. I look forward to
your feedback.

Also, I will be in London on the 9th, and am
hoping I can join you at the gymnastics club.
When do you think you'll be going, morning or
afternoon?

Looking forward to hopefully seeing you there.

Becky

***

[*March 2021, Teams video call*]

Becky is waiting, looking at the screen, the steam rising from her mug, her favourite tea brewing. She wonders what Fran's reaction to the finished roughs will be. Has she 'got it'? Was she able to capture and translate the essence of the story Fran entrusted her to portray?

"Becky, thank you so much for sharing the finished roughs! I love them!" Fran's enthusiasm pierces the screen.

"Haha, I am glad to hear this… and they are not completely finished yet, I mean, did you notice page 3? I need to update it, it's from the first ever draft I did, before we went to London and observed the training. When I look at those drawing, I am so glad we managed to go to the club before the pandemic started!" (see Figure 11.2).

"Wow, I hadn't really noticed so much, but you are right…look at it. Trudy is so different. And the number of details in the scene…"

"Yeah, I think I must have modelled the coach partly on Margarita Mamun's coach in *Over the Limit*, and partly on a slightly 'manly' female P.E. teacher stereotype. One of the interesting things about going to draw in the gym was to see how young the coaches were – that they were all women who did not look much older than the oldest gymnasts there."

Figure 11.1 Becky's first draft after reading the creative nonfiction.

"…and then you asked me to send you my description of Trudy and Sally, to see what I was picturing when I was writing them…"

"Yes. The description of Trudy you sent me was also quite different to the images I'd already made and formed in my mind. The pictures of Sally didn't surprise me as much – perhaps her appearance and the seriousness of one of the photos at least related to what I'd been imagining."

Figure 11.2 Becky's final work, after observing a training session in person.

Fran chuckles. "It's funny, the ethnography was based on observation, but just talking to you made me realise I never really paid attention to how they actually *looked*. I guess when I was writing my focus had been on communicating feelings and thoughts, but not appearance."

"Fair point. You didn't need that back then probably. We can now say this is something we learnt from our collaboration: one more dimension added in the translation from written word to comic."

The Relationship between Words and Images

"Talking about layers, I have to say that my favourite page is probably the one where you showed Trudy's thoughts, where in the CNF she thinks, '[...] everything seems to be going wrong today! Some of the younger gymnasts have started crying, whilst the older gymnasts are complaining of pain here and there.'[1] I mean, when I saw the comic, it really answers the *show rather than tell* mantra of creative nonfiction.[2] And…I don't know, I just found the way you showed the relationship very powerful. That balance between good and bad, caring/uncaring that I paid so much attention to when writing the story. The fact that I didn't want to simply paint Trudy as the bad one. I think you really got that by showing her interacting differently with different gymnasts. That conversation with the tiny gymnast, those words, 'go wash your face'…that's such a classic scene in gymnastics. I guess some would call it 'gaslighting,' but in general it is the perfect representation of a culture that only cares up to a point and doesn't have time for more.[3] And to see it there, in your drawings… its power really took me by surprise" (see Figure 11.3).

"I am so relieved to hear this! It's the page where I took most artistic license in adding information that didn't feature in your written story."

"It's really interesting actually. It's like you are creating images for Trudy's stream of consciousness. Is it, like, a method of drawing comics?"

"Well, it *was* actually an interesting page to work on: I wanted to use parts of Trudy's inner monologue as the text, so that the reader would know her frustration, and I also saw the potential to use pictures alongside that text to show what she was describing – the things that are prompting her frustrated thoughts. In comics, the panels are moments in time – "boxes of time," as Hilary Chute[4] puts it – so by distributing a character's thoughts across a sequence of panels, those thoughts are anchored to the events in those panels. The thoughts could be read as simultaneous with the actions, or else as visual memories connected to the thoughts. I wanted to go a step further, though, and use the comics' potential for drama to drop the reader into a direct exchange between Trudy and one of the younger gymnasts who has started crying. That was inspired in part by a conversation between a coach and a gymnast that I overheard during the training session I observed in London."

Fran listens to Becky, hoping her expression is able to convey – even through a screen – how in awe she feels. *This is it* – she cannot help but think – *exactly what I needed to make my story more 'usable': layers of communication, visual, written…this can be really powerful. I wonder what gymnasts will feel when reading it…."*

Figure 11.3 Example of translation from words to images.

"Becky, this is amazing! So powerful, thank you... I can't wait to use this comic to work with gymnasts!"

Representation of Pain in Writing and in Images

"What do you think about the various attempts at drawing pain? Is there anything that speaks to you more clearly? Anything that you prefer me to use?"

RIIING! RIIING!

"Becky, I'm sorry! Just another delivery. I'll be back in a sec!"

Becky smiles, of course...we are all getting used to working from home these days...she keeps looking at the pain drawings she has on her second screen...will they work? Are they good enough? *"This whole drawing pain has been quite the challenge...pain is such a subjective feeling.*[5] *I never had to draw a story where it's important that the reader gets an insight into the physical experience of a character..."*

"I'm back! Sorry again!" Fran jumps back on the screen again. "You were saying...? Oh yes, the pain! I mean, I am really not sure if my comments can be of any help here, because I was literally amazed by the pictures of Sally in pain. It seemed so – pass me this comment, I'll explain – *easy*. What I mean is that the use of red...the moment I saw that page where she is doing the double skips with the rope as punishment, and her back pain starts flaring up... You have no idea how long we worked on finding different metaphors for pain when writing the CNF![6] I went crazy! The knife, the burning sensation, the animal creeping up the spine...anything. And yes, they were evocative descriptions, I hope. But then, one look at the page you drew and that red line running through her back was so immediate! I love how with just one stroke, one colour, the comic can represent all those words, all those metaphors. I had never considered before how well drawing can communicate embodied feelings.[7] But then, I remember reading that the form we use to recount pain affects one's reaction to that encounter,[8] and while the book where I read this focused on different literary genres, I wonder how it applies to visual forms."

"Wow, that's an interesting question... individuals' reaction to how we portray pain. Funny, I guess for me it is important to create an empathetic response in the reader without relying too much on the kind of grimaces and exaggerated body-language that we're perhaps used to seeing in imagery that should communicate 'this person is in pain.' You know, like adverts for back pain, for example."

"Mm hm, yes, I think I know what you mean. Those people with their hands on their backs, faces distorted by pain...It makes sense you want something more subtle, refined maybe?"

"Yes. I mean, those images are part of a shared visual language, at a cultural level – and of course, we are social animals who can read pain in the face of another person and respond with sympathy.[9] But to me, when drawing a story, the most important thing is to do it in a way that draws the reader in to the protagonists' experience. Although they are watching it from the outside, the way it is told and drawn should invite them to imaginatively inhabit these characters and understand how they are feeling. And, thinking of your story, I'd like to bring the reader as close as possible to Sally's experience. I want them to occupy the first-person perspective that your story offers the reader. In its written form, we are given access to Sally and Trudy's thoughts and feelings in turn. I am trying to find visual metaphors that can achieve this."

"That would be using the red, right?"

"Yes, I resorted to using red as it's the colour that's most immediately associated with violence, with physical injury, with danger and warning. Also, in English pain is often described as being 'like a red-hot poker'."

"Aw, I wonder how it is possible that I missed that metaphor in my CNF! Ha-ha! But yes, I get what you mean, red also connects to fire, and the expression of 'burning pain' comes to mind. That was definitely what I thought the moment I saw your first sketch."

"Yes, and that obviously works well. But now I tried something else too. Let me share my screen and I can show you."

While Becky clicks away to be able to show Fran what she means, they both sigh, longing for those lively coffee chats they had in person until a few months ago.

"Can you see my screen?"

"Yep!"

"So, on this page here, as well as the red, I tried to use the way I was making marks in these drawings to suggest the aggressive quality of the pain (see Figure 11.4). Scott McCloud – remember, the author I told you about, who wrote about storytelling and visual communication? – he talks about this, the way that "all lines carry [...] an expressive potential."[10] There's a chapter in the book you recommended, *Dimensions of Pain*,[11] that focuses on the different ways we use to visualise pain.[12] I loved reading how the author discusses the various strategies in pain metaphors."

"That chapter only looks at written work though, right?"

"It does, yes, but still it was interesting for me – communicating with images – to read his analysis. I became more aware of the different strategies in written and visual art to convey pain. For example, in your story, pain has agency and seems to attack from the outside. In my translation to images, it's an internal force. I wonder whether I should find a way to externalise the pain in the comic, to be truer to your original story?"

"I am not sure…I mean, to me the images you are using are so effective in communicating pain. As you said, this is a translation, isn't it? When you translate from one language to another, the best translation is not always a literal one. Maybe it is the same when translating from words to images?"

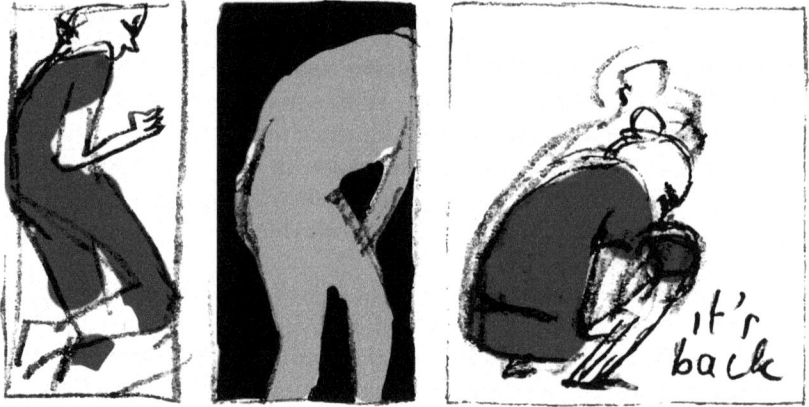

Figure 11.4 Becky's experiments for communicating pain through aggressive marks.

"I think you are right…this is a translation, after all. And probably this is the perfect example of the shift that has to happen moving from one medium to another."

"Yes, I think it makes sense. In a way it is like when we were discussing our projects with the students and that master's student asked that question that threw us a little… remember?"

"How could I forget? The one who wanted to know, 'where is the data?'…"

Where is the data?

[*August 2020*]

From: Cavallerio, Francesca

To: Palmer, Becky

Attachment: Study 1- Results _ updated.pdf
Hello!
I literally can't wait to see the
transformation into the comic, and of course
I am open to an adaptation for the visual
version… The important aspect for me is to
still communicate the themes from my findings.
The majority of the dialogue in the story
is taken from interviews, so if we use that
in the comic, we are still representing
the participants' voices… So yes, for me

the rigour from a research perspective is
important, but when it comes to representing
it visually, you are the expert!
Just in case this can help, attached is the
document with the analysis following data
collection. You have the four main themes
identified, with a description for each of
them. I don't know if this helps, but these
were the themes I tried to represent through
the creative nonfiction. I thought maybe seeing
the phase before the story could help you too.
Speak soon!
Fran

From: Palmer, Becky

To: Cavallerio, Francesca

Hey Fran,
I just read through the presentation you
sent, with the themes from your analysis.
It's interesting to get this insight into
your results and the process of collecting
and analysing the data. And it will be useful
to have the themes in mind while I'm working
on the comic. When we get to the stage where
I can show you the roughs, we can discuss
whether they are coming across clearly enough.
I'm aiming to include all the dialogue, but
since there may be sections of internal
monologue that there isn't space for, it would
be good to talk about these parts at that
stage and see whether there are any that you
do want to keep as part of the text, or if
there's a way to emphasise/express them better
visually.
It would be great to meet up when you get
back!
Becky

***

[*December 2020 – online research seminar*]
  "...and so, this is an example of how you can represent research findings in ways that move beyond the 'classic' style you might be used to, and
even use different media. Any questions?"

Virtual clapping hands appear on the screens, Fran and Becky smile. They did it! They finally shared the work they have been doing over the past year! And hopefully they managed to show students (and colleagues) that there is more to research than just realist tales.[13]

A virtual hand is raised. The seminar chair calls the name of the student, a microphone is turned on: "Sorry, I was just wondering...after you adapted all this, where is the data? How can you be sure that what you represented is still the same data she collected?"

Both microphones on, the usual awkwardness of looking at each other, thinking *"Who goes first?"* Becky takes a small breath, and Fran relaxes back on her chair, on her side of the screen, knowing that Becky is thinking back to those emails, to all those conversations. She listens, while her colleague starts explaining.

"Thank you for your question, that's a fair point, something we asked ourselves a few times. First of all, Fran didn't just share the final product with me, but she gave me an insight into the analysis she conducted. For me it was so useful to read the results as they were *before* she wrote the story: it helped me focus on what was most important to get across in the comic, too. Because of the challenge of representing pain, that had come to dominate what I was thinking about in relation to the comic. But reading about the themes, I remembered that the pain wasn't the focus in itself. Yes, on one hand I had to communicate Sally's physical experience effectively for the reader to be really aware of the stress her body was under, but on the other hand the purpose of that was to draw attention to the 'culture of risk' and the normalisation of pain that it produces; and the miscommunication between coach and gymnast was clearly another key theme."

"Shall I jump in for a quick summary, as maybe not everyone remembers the original CNF?" Fran says. "Just to recap, so that what Becky is about to explain might be clearer, the 'lack of communication' theme was the most important to me. When I was doing the study, that absence of dialogue became a fundamental aspect of the psychosocial dynamics I observed. So, once I started writing the CNF I had to make sure that theme was not missed. After several attempts, with my supervisors we settled for what is the final version: not one story, but two. The gymnast's, and the coach's. Same training session, same events, different perspectives, different thoughts. My characters were close in one way, but almost worlds apart in another, and the best way to show that was by keeping their stories divided, running in parallel. So, I was surprised when I realised how the visual version of the story could be just that: *one* story."

The student's face is still unconvinced. *"Just let us finish!,"* thinks Fran.

"Let me explain what Fran means by this. I don't know if you noticed it when we showed you the comic, but if you think of the pages, you can see both characters, and as we said earlier, in the images you can merge thoughts and dialogue. This means that in the comic Sally and Trudy's stories are re-united, written as one. The training session goes back to being one training session, because the visual medium allowed me to still represent that miscommunication without the need for two separate stories. Yet, when it came to the end of the story, I worked differently (see Figure 11.5). You see, in comics scholarship, the layout of a page of comics is known as the 'page architecture.' Panels mark separate moments of time in a comic – at least this is how we learn to read them – but sometimes they are used to show different parts of a scene at the same moment. That kind of 'aspect-to-aspect' storytelling[14] is usually used to establish a mood, or an idea. So, when I drew the final page, the bottom two panels are both at the same time: we read them consecutively, but the thoughts of Trudy and Sally are happening simultaneously. The panel borders have become more than just a way to show time passing, it's a barrier between them, emphasising their separation."

"It was fascinating to see how at the end, the comic structure reflected the CNF again!," Fran burst out, incapable of containing her enthusiasm – Becky chuckles, it is so nice to see how much she loves her interpretation of the story.

"Yes, I agree. It's very satisfying how many ways there are to layer meaning into the building-blocks of comics and extend beyond their basic function to achieve an emotional impact like this. I hope this gave you a practical example of *where the data is*?"

"Yes, I think I see what you both mean," – says the student, sounding keener than before – "so you used the themes as a basis and a point of reference to make sure the story is true to the findings?"

"Yes, but then also allowing the reader to inhabit a situation where all these themes are interconnected, so that they can also understand how they interact with each other."

"Can I ask a follow-up question?" says a pompous voice.

Becky notices the slightly unenthusiastic look on Fran's face. She told her a colleague she is not a fan of was going to join the seminar – not because he particularly cared, but because his role required him to show his face. "Yes, of course," they reply in unison, thinking *"Let's see what he asks now."*

"You already decided to represent research findings through *[horrified tone of voice]* a story. And now you are telling us that "translating" it into a comic is still okay, it still makes it valid and reliable research?"

Breathe in. Breathe out.

"No, we are not."

Silence.

"Let me unpack my answer. The reason why I say this, is that I don't hold my CNF either to criteria of validity or reliability, simply because they do not apply to the interpretivist paradigm, which underpins this study.[15] The quality criteria we are using to judge the quality of this work are what we'd call relativist criteria.[16] Is the story evocative? Does it

Figure 11.5 Using panels' architecture to represent relationships.

resonate with its readers? Does it have an emotional or intellectual impact on them? Is it credible? Generally speaking, we know that visual images can enhance empathic understanding, they can make us pay attention to things in new ways, and they can communicate effectively because they incorporate multiple layers.[17] So, considering these aspects, I think we worked towards meeting those criteria. And I know some researchers will worry about the fact that there can be different interpretations to the comic, but that's a risk that goes with all forms of creative nonfiction.[18] A famous book by Arthur Frank is titled *Letting stories breathe*[19]: the same applies to visual stories like comics. An image – be it created with words or pen and ink – will constantly be part of a process of re-construction and re-interpretation.[20]

"Yes, I agree with Fran. It's one of the fundamental aspects of visual art. A quote I love says, 'What a specific image can mean or represent at any given time depends on a lot of factors, including who is doing the viewing and the context in which the image is viewed,'[21] which from my perspective is a strength of visual work, not a weakness. Drawings are also open about the fact that they were made: they don't pretend to be portraying objective truth in the way that photographs seem to."[22]

A virtual hand is raised, and a tiny voice tentatively starts. "Thank you, this was fascinating. Can I ask you something, though? You explained how the data for this project was collected, analysed, written up, and then transformed into visual. How do you think data collection for a research project like this might differ when a visual artist is involved as co-researcher from the beginning?"

Becky and Fran look at each other through the screen, smiling. Here's to the next shared project.

Final Thoughts

We wrote this chapter to give readers an insight into one way that research data represented using CNF can be translated into a visual story.[23] When we started this 'journey,' we could not have foreseen what the work would entail, nor the challenges we were going to encounter. In the story you have just read, we portrayed several aspects that were the focus of our collaboration:

- the visualisation of the environment to give a sense of place in the comic;
- exploring the relationship between words and images and its potential for conveying meaning in diverse ways;
- realising the difference in visual and written metaphors;
- ensuring our work was immersed in the data collected whilst allowing its development through the layers of analysis.

These should not be taken as a complete checklist to be ticked off. Naturally, each collaboration will be different, depending on many factors. One of these, as alluded to at the end of our story, is the point in the research at which the collaboration starts. Had we collected data to-gether, or analysed them in collaboration, the challenges would surely have differed. The subject matter itself will also influence the principal points of discussion, as will the particular approach taken in visualising the story. In addition, the age-group of the intended audience and the use envisaged for the outcome are likely to impact on the collaborators' focus. But we hope that highlighting the aspects which were key for us will provide others with food for thought when embarking on similar projects.

Acknowledgements

We would like to thank Isobelle Kennedy for her thoughtful feedback on the initial version of this chapter.

Notes

1 Cavallerio et al. (2016, p. 106).
2 Smith et al. (2016).
3 Stirling et al. (2020).
4 Chute (2010, p. 9).
5 McCaffery and Beebe (1989).
6 See Chapter 1 for more details on this point.
7 Gillies et al. (2005).
8 Mintz (2013).
9 Decety and Lamm (2006).
10 McCloud (1993, p. 124).
11 Käll (2012).
12 Biro (2012).
13 Sparkes (1995).
14 McCloud (1993, p. 79).
15 Smith and McGannon (2018).
16 Burke (2016).
17 Weber (2008).
18 Smith et al. (2016).
19 Frank (2010).
20 Weber (2008).
21 Weber (2008, p. 42).
22 Sacco (2012).
23 For readers interested in a visual version of this chapter, please go to https://visualstoriesaru.wordpress.com/a-day-at-training-collaborative-project/

References

Biro, D. (2012). When language runs dry: Pain, the imagination, and metaphor. In L. F. Käll (Ed.), *Dimensions of pain: Humanities and social science perspective*. Abingdon: Routledge.

Burke, S. (2016). Rethinking 'validity' and 'trustworthiness' in qualitative inquiry: How might we judge the quality of qualitative research in sport and exercise sciences. In B. Smith & A. C. Sparkes (Eds.), *Routledge handbook of qualitative research in sport and exercise* (pp. 330–339). Abingdon: Routledge.

Cavallerio, F., Wadey, R., & Wagstaff, C. R. (2016). Understanding overuse injuries in rhythmic gymnastics: A 12-month ethnographic study. *Psychology of Sport and Exercise, 25*, 100–109. https://doi.org/10.1016/j.psychsport.2016.05.002

Chute, H. (2010). *Graphic women: Life narrative & contemporary comics*. New York: Columbia University Press.

Crane-Williams, R. (2012). Can you picture this? *Visual Arts Research, 38*(1), 87–98.

Decety, J., & Lamm, C. (2006). Human empathy through the lens of social neuroscience. *The Scientific World Journal, 6*, 1146–1163. https://doi.org/10.1100/tsw.2006.221

Ellis, C. (2004). *The ethnographic I: A methodological novel about autoethnography*. Walnut Creek, CA: Rowman Altamira.

Foster, V. (2012). The pleasure principle: Employing arts-based methods in social work research. *European Journal of Social Work, 15*(4), 532–545. https://doi.org/10.1080/13691457.2012.702311

Frank, A. W. (2010). *Letting stories breathe: A socio-narratology*. Chicago, IL: University of Chicago Press.

Gair, S., & Van Luyn, A. (Eds.). (2016). *Sharing qualitative research: Showing lived experience and community narratives*. London: Routledge.

Galman, S. A. (2009). The truthful messenger: Visual methods and representation in qualitative research in education. *Qualitative Research, 9*(2), 197–217. https://doi.org/10.1177/1468794108099321

Gillies, V., Harden, A., Johnson, K., Reavey, P., Strange, V., & Willig, C. (2005). Painting pictures of embodied experience: The use of nonverbal data production for the study of embodiment. *Qualitative Research in Psychology, 2*(3), 199–212. https://doi.org/10.1191/1478088705qp038oa

Hackley, C. (2007). Auto-ethnographic consumer research and creative nonfiction. *Qualitative Market Research: An International Journal, 10*(1), 98–108. https://doi.org/10.1108/13522750710720422

Käll, L. F. (Ed.). (2012). *Dimensions of pain: Humanities and social science perspective*. Routledge

McCaffery, M., & Beebe, A. (1989). The numeric pain rating scale instructions. In N. W. Dolphin & B. L. Crue Jr (Eds.), *Pain: Clinical manual for nursing practice*. St. Louis, MO: Mosby.

McCloud, S. (1993). *Understanding comics: The invisible art*. New York: HarperCollins.

Mintz, S. B. (2013). *Hurt and pain: Literature and the suffering body*. London: Bloomsbury Publishing.

Smith, B., & McGannon, K. R. (2018). Developing rigor in qualitative research: Problems and opportunities within sport and exercise psychology. *International Review of Sport and Exercise Psychology, 11*(1), 101–121. https://doi.org/10.1080/1750984X.2017.1317357

Smith, B., McGannon, K. R., & Williams, T. L. (2016). Ethnographic creative nonfiction. In G. Molnár & L. Purdy (Eds.), *Ethnographies in sport and exercise research* (pp. 49–73). Abingdon: Routledge.

Sparkes, A.C. (1995). Writing people: Reflections on the dual crises of representation and legitimation in qualitative inquiry. *Quest, 47*(2), 158–195. https://doi.org/10.1080/00336297.1995.10484151

Stirling, A., Tam, A., Milne, A., & Kerr, G. (2020). Media narratives of gymnasts' abusive experiences: Keep smiling and pointing your toes. In R. Kerr,

N. Barker-Ruchti, C. Stewart, & G. Kerr (Eds.), *Women's artistic gymnastics: Socio-cultural perspectives* (pp. 81–99). Abingdon: Routledge.

Thomas, G. (2012). Thinking inside the boxes: The importance of comics and graphic novels in visual arts education. *Visual Arts Research, 38*(1), 64–86.

Weber, S. (2008). Visual images in research. In G. Knowles & A. Cole (Eds.), *Handbook of the arts in qualitative research* (pp. 41–54). Thousand Oaks, CA: Sage.

Weber, W., & Rall, H. M. (2017). Authenticity in comics journalism. Visual strategies for reporting facts. *Journal of Graphic Novels and Comics, 8*(4), 376–397. https://doi.org/10.1080/21504857.2017.1299020

Index

Note: **Bold** page numbers refer to tables, *italic* page numbers refer to figures and page numbers followed by "n" refer to end notes.

9 781032 120164